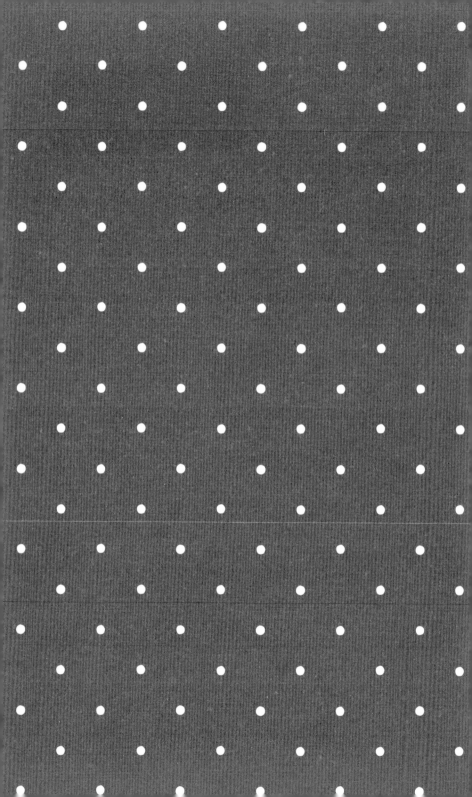

dream

plan

& go

RACHEL McMILLAN

ARTWORK by LAURA L. BEAN

HARVEST HOUSE PUBLISHERS
EUGENE, OREGON

Cover and interior design by Studio Gearbox

Some of the names have been changed to protect others' privacy.

Dream, Plan, and Go

Text copyright © 2020 by Rachel McMillan, artwork copyright © 2020 by Laura L. Bean
Published by Harvest House Publishers
Eugene, Oregon 97408
www.harvesthousepublishers.com

ISBN 978-0-7369-7969-6 (pbk.)
ISBN 978-0-7369-7970-2 (eBook)

Library of Congress Cataloging-in-Publication Data is on file at the Library of Congress,
Washington, DC.

Printed in South Korea

20 21 22 23 24 25 26 27 28 / FCSK / 10 9 8 7 6 5 4 3 2 1

FOR MY SISTER,

LEAH,

WHO LOVINGLY MAKES

THE WORLD A SMALLER PLACE

Contents

Finding Your Own Adventure

Adventure is worthwhile in itself.

AMELIA EARHART

*F*or centuries, to uphold her reputation and be acceptable in polite society, a woman couldn't be seen in public without a suitable companion. In the film *Miss Potter*, author and illustrator Beatrix Potter can't meet with her publisher without a chaperone. In *A Room with a View*, Lucy Honeychurch's cousin, Charlotte Bartlett, must accompany her to see the ruins and grandeur of Italy.

Today, though, women can venture to a local performance or restaurant alone without drawing attention to themselves. Not only that, but they can see the whole of the world on their own. Yet how often do they take the opportunity to wander a foreign city or even see a movie or a play or check out a restaurant without a companion?

When was the last time you took yourself out on a date—if ever?

Not only do I think we should take advantage of our freedom as women in an age when being in only our own company is acceptable, but I believe we should embrace the adventures we can find near and far.

While it's necessary to be aware of the challenges of being a solo woman—especially when traveling—and while precautions and common sense must direct our opportunities, those opportunities are endless. When I talk to women about my passion for going out into the world alone, whether near or far, I commonly hear many of them say they're waiting for a boyfriend or husband—a perfect man, a perfect partnered opportunity—to experience what interests them both locally and abroad. I confess, until I was in my late twenties, this was very much at the forefront of my mind too, which is why no one was more surprised than I was when I took myself on a honeymoon to Vienna.

No More Waiting

The Billy Joel song I had loved since childhood prom- ised Vienna was waiting for me, but I no longer wanted to wait for it. I'd been waiting since I was ten years old, the splendid Austrian capital not only my dream city but also my dream honeymoon destination. I wanted to experience the scents of pastries from the Demel Konditorei spilling onto the cobblestones of Kohlmarkt. The bells of Stephansdom, the cathedral towering over the city, tolling among the shoppers on the Graben's pedestrian walkway. Manicured green shrubs bordering the Kunsthistorisches Museum while music from the Musikverein concert hall and the Staatsoper opera house flooded over a city once home to the greatest composers of the Baroque and Classical periods.

In my imagination, no place in the world could hold a candle to the opulent city ornamented by the grandeur of the Hapsburg Empire of long ago. As a hopeless romantic with the dream of visiting a hopelessly romantic city, I determined my dashing prince would be as excited to play "ring around the Ringstrasse," the circular boulevard at the center of Vienna's famed first district, as I was. We would ramble under buttery-tinted rooftops and explore Mozarthaus Vienna museum and eat Sachertorte, the famously rich chocolate cake named for the hotel. I didn't even mind forgoing everything but a breakfast and a chamber orchestra made up of my friends from high school band if it meant our wedding funds could be transferred to a Viennese honeymoon.

Vienna waited through high school as I taped pictures from magazines on my locker door. It waited through college as backpacking friends sent me postcards I framed and placed in my bachelor apartment. Then in my late twenties, still single, a thought struck: What if I never married? What would happen to my idyllic Viennese honeymoon? If I didn't have a husband to take me to Vienna, would I *never* see Vienna? I decided I would go by the time I was 30. If Prince Charming showed up, fine. If not, I would purchase a German phrase book and set off solo. Vienna would wait no longer.

That first trip to Vienna became a symbol of my decision never to wait for a companion to pursue a dream—however big or small the scale. It can be intimidating for women to step out on our own and grab at a chance. It can be discouraging to tweak a desired dream when life doesn't work out the way we planned, when the errant prince doesn't show up or the best friend who had been so keen on a trip together is now bound to family obligations.

I spent my first time in Austria during a stickily hot summer week with a journal under my arm and a caffeinated excitement attributed to my determination to try at least a dozen different kinds of coffee. I didn't have a man by my side, and the

trip wasn't a celebration of my marriage, but I was drenched in romantic moments. I courted a city steeped in history while fumbling my way through hiccupped German words that sat awkwardly in my Canadian accent.

A lovely young man named Klaus, described in an email to my sister as having "sun-licked brown hair," saved me from lugging my suitcase aimlessly around the Museumsquartier, a gorgeous green span populated by every museum imaginable. I had confused the street *Breitgasse* with the street *Breitsgasse*, the latter home to my hotel. I used the recommendations he wrote in my Moleskine notebook to fall into Vienna's rhythm, which emulated the three-quarter time popularized by its famous waltz. I sampled Sachertorte and attended concerts and lost myself down alleyways and through the grand gardens of Schönbrunn Palace and Schloss Belvedere, another fairy-tale palace.

Vienna was poetry to me. I couldn't fathom how a companion would have enriched the experience. I saved for it. I worked for it. I went with my own itinerary and desire in mind. I *appreciated* it.

I appreciated it even more on the patio of Café Mozart in the Albertinaplatz, a central square, on a sunny, hot day. Sipping Einspanner, a delectable mélange of strong espresso and whipped cream, and scribbling in my journal, I was surprised when a fashionable lady tossed her rainbow scarf over her tailored outfit and, in broken English, asked if she could join me.

I closed my journal and motioned for this Austrian woman to take a seat. She placed her tiny espresso cup and dainty dessert on my table and then studied me with watery-blue eyes.

"You are not American." Her tone hovered between a statement and a question.

"Canadian," I replied.

"May I practice my English on you?"

Her English far surpassed my choppy German. She spoke of her husband, who had passed away a few months before. Visiting Canada had been their dream as they read about the mountains and lakes, moose and maple trees. She spoke of my home country while my eyes wandered over the architecture of the Staatsoper and the Albertina Museum, each like too much whipped cream in their ornamentation. She and her husband had practiced English together so they could plan the trip. Then he was gone. She put her hand over mine. "I will never see Canada now."

My coffee sat untouched when she left me in my glorious honeymoon city alone with my journal and jet lag.

It wasn't until much later, insomnia drawing me to reruns of *Frasier* in dubbed German, that I let myself be frustrated on her behalf. My elegant Austrian lady would never find her moose and maple trees. Her husband was gone, and that was that. I reached for my journal and scribbled *She should go anyway.*

Heart Places

My first trip to Austria not only inspired several subsequent solo trips but also fueled my passion to encourage women to seek adventures across the sea or in their own backyard whether or not they have someone with whom they can experience them. It also encouraged me to be attuned to my own heart places. Everyone has them. Space of the universe you feel you may have met before. A house or a hotel or a stretch of land for which your heart feels ownership and an affinity. Again, these corners of the world may not lie across the ocean; they might be in our own backyards. They can often be found merely by opening our eyes, taking a few moments to compare what we know about ourselves with a surrounding unfolding before us.

So often I meet women who are uncomfortable eating in a restaurant or seeing a film alone. Certainly, we can experience nerves when we think we're standing out, but the freedom realized once this fear is alleviated opens up our world. It can also inspire us to think deeply about the authenticity of our connections and acquaintances. Have you ever found yourself inviting someone to a movie or to the theater or to dinner not because you especially wanted the company but because you didn't want to go solo?

Learning not only how to be comfortable alone but also *happy* when alone can seem to go against the grain of everything society normalizes. We live in an age of constant connection. We wake up and immediately check social media. We create a persona online and allow people so "close" that they know what we had for dinner (through a carefully filtered photo, of course). We put high emphasis on finding the perfect friend groups—and the one person meant for us.

Human connection is wonderful; so are friendships and romantic relationships. But we don't often cultivate nor are we taught being alone. Yet I believe knowing how to be alone is essential. To be satisfied and content alone is a wonderful gift. It allows you to observe and sense what you might not if you were in the company of other people.

It's okay to think about yourself in the name of self-discovery. It's okay to acknowledge that you want to get to know yourself as well as you know your family and friends. And it's still okay that a man might intercept you while you're living your own happily ever after. My going to Vienna didn't symbolize my shutting the door to conventional romance or the opportunity for a someday companion. Rather, it heightened my love of romance in all manner of forms, from travel to art to music to food.

Recently, I read a piece on writer Anne Lamott's nuptials in the Vows section of the *New York Times*. At 65, Lamott was getting married for the first time. When asked what she would tell women wondering about finding eventual companionship, she said, "If you're paying attention and making your own life as beautiful and rich and as fun as it can be, you might just attract someone who's doing the same thing."[1] In other words, don't wait. Keep living your life. Put nothing on hold.

Romance can be found in a concert by a local orchestra, in the first bite of dessert at a bakery, or in an evening ramble along the boardwalk during a summer fair. I believe women—single or married—should consider making the effort to pursue what they love... unaccompanied. It's wonderful to share experiences with friends or family or on a date with a dashing man, but why be afraid to spend time with just yourself as well?

Obligation to fill silence? Not a problem. The expectation to comment on or agree with someone else's reaction to an event? Irrelevant. A compromised and debated itinerary? Your time is your own. Alone, you make your own

---

1 Lois Smith Brady, "The Writer Anne Lamott Gets to the Happily-Ever-After Part," https://www.nytimes .com/2019/04/26/fashion/weddings/the-final-chapters-of-anne-lamotts-life-now-include-a-soul-mate .html?searchResultPosition=1.

"IF YOU'RE PAYING
ATTENTION AND
MAKING YOUR OWN
LIFE AS BEAUTIFUL
AND RICH AND AS
FUN AS IT CAN BE,
YOU MIGHT JUST
ATTRACT SOMEONE
WHO'S DOING THE
SAME THING."

adventure at your own pace, and you might get to know yourself in a new way. "You are who you are when you are alone," my youth group pastor often reminded us.

For married women with families, it might look a little different to grab at some adventures because of the responsibilities of day-to-day life, but I hope *Dream, Plan, and Go* will help you, too, find opportunities to carve out moments for yourself, chances to find those heart places your children and husband might not share but, I hope, will be happy for you to explore.

You have the dream, whether it's to linger by yourself over a cupcake at a local bakery while your Saturday responsibilities wait a while or to tack two extra days onto a work trip to visit a historical site. Or you might be single and crave the freedom to attend that high school graduation or friend's destination wedding without the expectation of a plus one. You deserve the chance to be a woman alone. I am hopeful that some of my anecdotes will inspire you to step out and find a new corner of your world. For while some of the names have been changed, each experience is relayed as authentically as possible—as if I were sitting across from you swapping stories of my adventures.

But you also might need permission to see it through. To go with no stress over a declined invite, no anxiety because you're the only one with the means or vacation

time while your friends and family are otherwise preoc-
cupied. So consider this book your permission form.

And I'm not just talking about the sweeping dreams
that color the corners of our minds, rebalance our bud-
gets, and take years of planning—but the smaller ones
too. Enjoy the anticipation and fulfillment of all kinds
of adventures—both the ones that send us across the sea
and the ones that encourage us to be tourists in our own
backyard.

Steps to Confidence

- Do you have a piece of jewelry, a favorite top, or a kind of makeup you save for special occasions because it makes you feel your best? Take it with you. (Mine is red lipstick, so I always have it when I travel.)

- You may feel intimidated if you're in a place where you don't speak the language. But remember, communication doesn't always require words. You can make eye contact with the person you're engaging with and smile.

- View your adventure as an investment, because you are an investment. You might lie awake pondering your financial obligations, but you'll have more confidence if you stop second-guessing every single expenditure. You've budgeted for the trip or event; now enjoy it.

- You may feel out of place, under- or overdressed, or that you stick out because you're alone somewhere. But people are too busy to stare and care. Think about how often you're in public without paying attention to the people around you in any deep, memorable way. Do you forever remember the woman at the grocery store who dropped her bags? Do you spend hours mulling over the tourist who bumped into you on the street? Stop believing that people are staring at you and immediately heighten your confidence.

- You're not required to be friendly to everyone you meet, especially if it makes you feel exposed or uncomfortable. You have every right to excuse yourself from an unwanted conversation on a plane and put on your headphones. You have every right to decline the gentleman who wants to pull up a seat at your café table. You have every right to open your journal during the group tour and decline talking to your seatmate. Do all that with confidence.

- Confidence comes in knowing what you want. This is your adventure. How did it play out in your dreams? Make that happen as close as possible in reality.

Think back to the first place you imagined visiting as a child.
Is that dream destination—an event or a festival or amusement
park—the same in adulthood? Maybe even visiting another
country? What does it tell you about yourself?

....

....

....

....

....

....

....

....

....

Talk to the people in your life about what their childhood dream trip was. How does it differ from yours? Or do you have that dream in common?

CHAPTER ONE

The Formative Adventure

Believe you can and you're halfway there.

THEODORE ROOSEVELT

Confidence doesn't live in one arena; it travels. And the confidence you can find in sojourning alone—near or far—can translate to other aspects of your life. Buying your own train ticket and navigating to the platform can be what you remember before a difficult exam. Finding your way out of a wrong turn without asking directions can give you the feeling of empowerment you need to apply for that new job. Ordering from a menu not in your language and then savoring and enjoying the food can be what you remember as you face a difficult interview question. Life experiences often help us find the courage we need in other areas.

For me, building that confidence—and the confidence to adventure on my own—started both early and close to home.

As I was finishing high school, I made a list of things

I wanted to do in and near my Canadian hometown of Orillia before I left to begin the next chapter of my life. I wanted to ensure that I didn't miss out on anything. These weren't magnanimous adventures nor expensive plans. For instance, I had always wanted to peer inside a particular antique furniture store and to wander at a local museum for a day. I wanted to have a picnic in Bala, Muskoka, a village about 40 minutes from my home, and to spend several days writing at a small café table at Mariposa Market, a favorite place in small Orillia. And I planned to do all this alone.

Whenever I talk to people who've had the courage to embark on adventures, I usually find this common denominator: Someone inspired them to go. For me, this person was my aunt Annette.

The summer before I left for college, my mom and I visited her in London, Ontario, just as she was prepping for her own solo adventure. When we arrived, her bike and helmet were already in the front hallway, and she gave us the "wait a minute" finger as she ordered a favorite takeout panzerotti from a neighborhood restaurant. I saw a map of Quebec on her dining room table as well as notes in her distinctive hand, plotting her trip. Bon Jovi's "It's My Life" was blaring from the CD player.

"It's my theme this summer," she told me.

She had mapped out bike routes in rural Quebec and planned to spend time in gorgeously historic Quebec City. Quebec City is a fortified city, dating back more than 400 years, whose architecture and landscape make one feel as if they're peeling back the curtain of time. And anytime I'm fortunate to visit the walled old quarter, it's like stepping into Europe.

I realized my aunt's planning her solo adventure perfectly intersected my preparations for moving away and being on my own. I was at a turning point.

Throughout my life, I've been fortunate to be inspired by friends and family members who grab at chances. Sometimes that has involved an adventure like climbing Mount Kilimanjaro—as my sister, Leah, did—and sometimes that's involved a woman going to see something like a Sunday afternoon documentary—alone. And because of that kind of inspiration, I embarked on my first true solo adventure—a second semester of school in England.

Learning to Be Me

The opportunity to spend a semester abroad not only opened up the world to me in a new way but also kickstarted my lifelong passion for independent travel. I wasn't nervous about spending time in a foreign country, meeting new friends, or the arduous syllabus and readings condensed to ensure we got full credits in shortened semesters. But to *get* to England, I would have to get airborne.

I would have to get on a plane.

For a split second, I considered abandoning the whole thing.

My carry-on in one hand and a small bottle of prescribed anxiety pills in the other, terrified of enclosed spaces and heights, my trek across the ocean required my being strapped into a seat in a small, bus-like circumference thousands of feet in the air.

Somehow (shakily), I boarded. Somehow (shakily), I swallowed my pill with a glass of water from a flight attendant, and somehow (shakily), I survived. Then, high above England, I looked out the window, down over a patchwork of green fields and lightly rolling hills so different from the farmland in Canada. When I was later brave enough to get on another plane—again alone—something in me had shifted. This time I stepped over my uncertainty and conquered a fear not everyone suffers.

Once there, email was my only form of electronic communication, although I funneled my unending thoughts on many of the books I read on LiveJournal. My cell phone had only one function: making and receiving phone calls. I had time, then, to put into practice what I had just started learning during my first semester in Toronto. I was learning how to be *me* away from the friends, family, and connections that made up so much of my life.

England was a good starting point to adjust to a first foreign experience because, although it was in a different time zone and an ocean away from home, the country had a similar culture and the people spoke the same language. But I quickly learned that some of the other exchange students were happy to spend their resources and free time clubbing in Brighton or shopping for cheap clothes in London. I realized, then, that if I wanted to get the most out of this once-in-a-lifetime experience, I had to do so solo. Without this sudden bravery, which rivalled my determination to face my fear of flying, I might not have found the courage to navigate this new world.

Before I'd left, my brother, Jared, had cut through the advice, concerns, and apprehension of many of my friends and family. He pulled me aside and said, "You're smarter than you think. And more street savvy than people realize." Sometimes you just need one person to believe you have courage so you can find reserves of it.

I thought about the alone times I'd had before. I recalled when a play called *Sherlock's Last Case* was playing at the theater in my hometown. I was 15, and this wasn't exactly the hot ticket for kids my age. But I was a die-hard Sherlock Holmes fan, so I bought a ticket. My dad dropped me off a half hour early so I could pick up a few books at the neighboring public library.

It was the first evening I'd ever felt truly grown up, signing out books and then wandering over to the theater in my dress and polished shoes.

At intermission, I read my program, studying it intently. I also realized I could live with the scrutiny I might experience as a solo teenager in a crowd of mostly older patrons. After that, if a historical movie or Gilbert and Sullivan play came to town, I didn't worry about frantically calling my school or youth group friends in hopes of aligning my unique interests with theirs. I tucked a book into my purse and went.

Conquering a lifelong fear of flying, my brother's belief in me, and recalling times I had successfully navigated alone were just the inspiration I needed to try more experiences alone. Once in England, then, I lined up for half-price tickets at the Leicester Square booth in the West End Tube station and saw musicals—alone. I maneuvered my way to the Falmer train station and navigated the transfers that would take me to Portsmouth—alone. I had always wanted to go to Portsmouth to seek out the ships and coast I had admired through my fervent reading of Patrick O'Brian's seafaring series and my love of C.S. Forester's Horatio Hornblower. I ordered a pint at the Eagle and Child pub in Oxford, where Lewis and Tolkien and Dorothy L. Sayers talked about fiction and theology, and I sought out the battlefields of Hastings, a castled village green looking over the choppy sea.

The semester was the perfect balance of planned activities and classwork as I worked toward credits in history and Shakespeare amid the excitement of being across the world in the birthplace of the books and history that had been a million points of reference for me since I was a little kid.

Alone, I took the double-decker from Victoria Station to Baker Street and called my parents from the corner of a street where I finally and excitedly spotted the Sherlock Holmes Museum. Alone, I sought out Dover Castle and peered over the White Cliffs of Dover immortalized in the song. Alone, I walked along the pier at Brighton and just listened to the roar of the ocean.

Taking in the enormity of the Atlantic, unable to see anything but horizon straight out across the blue, I had wonderful conversations with myself. My journal was full of thoughts on everything from the Shakespeare I was learning to my disbelief that an entire world could be so full of a history other than Canada's. The oldest buildings in my life were from the eighteenth century at the earliest. Here, the patchwork green and rolling hills were interrupted by ruins, thatch-roofed cottages, and cathedrals that stood centuries, telling tales that sewed up their story and craftsmanship.

It was the first trip I learned to use a fake name as it made me feel a little less exposed. There's a balance you find traveling alone in being polite and firm rather than running away. Giving a made-up name assures confidence but still allows anonymity. It was the first time I found my way out of a crowded pub overrun with rowdy guys watching football, separating myself from my companions while dressed in a borrowed dress to look more like I was ready for the club than the library.

My ferry trip from Dover to Calais, France, recalled the pages of *The Scarlet Pimpernel* describing the route Sir Percy Blakeney took disguised as a wealthy clothes-obsessed fop to save aristocrats from the guillotine. In Dieppe, in the coastal Normandy region of France, my high school history textbooks came alive as I wandered the beaches where Canadian soldiers had fought, and I met with proprietors of a bed-and-breakfast who served me croissants and coffee and thanked my country profusely. And in Rouen along the Seine, I wandered through the narrow, cobbled streets and found the tower where Joan of Arc was held before her trial and execution and that the painter Claude Monet captured in the late nineteenth century. I ate cheese and watched the sun spill over lapping water.

I was far from home, and yet I was being introduced to a new, self-sufficient Rachel for the first time. I had gained a sense of who she was when I first waved good-bye to my mom and dad and closed the door of my university dorm room, but she couldn't fling herself to a different country and navigate all this.

The first adventure you take determines much of what you seek on subsequent adventures, but it also allows you to discover your strengths and how you're most comfortable.

Once I knew I could spend time away from family and friends with no immediate contacts in a foreign country, once I knew I could navigate a new world and board a train and leave on a ferry to France and figure out a foreign currency that wasn't the American currency familiar from some cross-border trips in my childhood, I wondered what else I could do. Could I take the bravery I'd gained and capitalize on it? Could I continue to straighten my shoulders and face the London subway and the maze of a new city? If I could do this, what else could I accomplish?

Taking First Steps

Now, I know not everyone shares delight in going somewhere solo. But it's a wonderful skill to have and to hone

"THE FIRST ADVENTURE YOU TAKE DETERMINES MUCH OF WHAT YOU SEEK ON SUBSEQUENT ADVENTURES."

for those moments when perhaps you *won't* have a travel companion. For those adventures, you need to take advantage of your own company. Trust me. Practicing solo adventure—even for an hour or two while on a trip with someone else—is a perfect way to slowly acclimate to being on your own.

For a young college student, the formative adventure might not mean crossing the Atlantic Ocean to study on another continent. It might be exploring a farmer's market a bus trip away from the dorm or visiting a restaurant near campus rather than reaching for the takeout menu.

But formative adventures certainly don't have to be the adventure taken on the cusp of adulthood. We're always learning and growing, but time alone can give our brains and hearts a welcome change and a chance for discovery.

Perhaps it's a day trip after your children have left home and you have more free time just for you. It could be an overnight adventure as you readjust to life after leaving a career. After the death of a loved one, time away can support a period of reflection as you begin to formulate ways to cope with the loss.

A change of scenery and the challenge of adventure can help us all clear our heads, reset, and gain fresh perspective.

Even if you reach an epoch of bravery, travel and adventuring don't necessarily become any easier or less intimidating. Once one hurdle is climbed, we tend to face another and another. But there is something wonderful in small victories and in finding strength in moments conquered. For you, this might be dining alone without a companion to act as a barrier between you and the people around you. It might mean sitting in a church pew by yourself when your husband or family is under the weather. No metric determines one act of bravery is braver than another; its worth is dependent on each person and each act of daring. Whatever is brave for you is *enough*. Don't discount the steps you take—small and large—to find your own adventure and gain confidence.

HISTORICAL SNAPSHOT

*W*hen Britain declared war on Germany in September 1939, Canadians immediately followed as obedient colonials. In 1942, while they still fought overseas, Operation Jubilee, also known as the Raid of Dieppe, was strategized. More than 6,000 infantrymen, the majority of which were Canadian, raided German-occupied France. Many were captured as prisoners of war, and many lost their lives on the beaches and at sea and in the air. To this day, citizens of Dieppe remember and honor the Canadians for their sacrifice in an attempt to end the war and liberate them.

Conquering the Fear of Flying

- A first major trip by plane should be taken after a practice round or two. Before traveling to somewhere across the world, start on a smaller scale by flying within your own state or country.

- Nerves before flying are common and shouldn't be taken lightly. Consult your doctor if you think medication might make the flight experience more bearable.

- Hydrate before the flight and on the plane—but avoid caffeine and alcohol. Both can heighten nerves, anxiety, and restlessness. Also get up and move around during any long or overnight flight to keep your circulation flowing.

- Opt for an aisle seat when you can. You won't feel as closed in.

- Start a good book, downloaded movie, or Netflix episode in the boarding area. You might be so engrossed and eager to continue the story that you'll fall into it on the plane and lose yourself in that world.

- Familiarize yourself with the plane, the attendants, and the sounds around you. Fear is exacerbated with the unknown, and most flight attendants are willing to calmly walk you through what you need to know.

- Distract yourself. Read your guidebook, consult your itinerary, or write about your travel experience in your journal retrospectively, detailing the challenges you overcame.

- One way to calm your nerves and slow a racing heart is a simple breathing exercise you can do in your seat (or just about anywhere). Take in a slow breath for three seconds, hold for three seconds, and release for three seconds. You can do this as many times as you need to, and it will focus your mind on something other than being nervous about being in a plane. Best of all, it's discreet, and it will make you feel better.

JOURNALING JUMP-STARTS

What did you think your first adventure would be?

....

....

....

How have other life experiences prepared you for a solo trip?

....

....

....

....

Has anyone in your life been the inspiration for an independent adventure?

....

....

....

....

What does travel mean to you? Does this come from an experience or a story you heard when you were young?

....

....

....

....

....

Is there a history of travel in your family tree?

....

....

....

How has the thread of your life led you to this opportunity for adventure?

....

....

....

....

....

....

CHAPTER TWO

The Adventure
Because of Others

*You can't stay in your corner of the forest
waiting for others to come to you.
You have to go to them sometimes.*

WINNIE-THE-POOH

ometimes traveling alone begins with a trip you take because of other people—family, friends, your boss. Maybe you didn't even have adventure in mind when the trip came up, but that didn't mean you couldn't take advantage of the chance to tack on some solo adventure.

Traveling because of other people has, for instance, taken me to San Francisco, where my friend Chelsea was looking for wedding dresses on a fun girls' weekend. It's taken me to beautiful Nanaimo on Vancouver Island in British Columbia, where my friend Sonja's wedding was in a gorgeous old barn designed to look like the most perfect, lavender-infused representation of Provincial France. Certainly, my work has taken me on travels, as have family events. And as much as possible, I've learned to slip in some solo adventuring as well.

Travel Because of Family and Friends

For a few years, while my closest friends were getting engaged and married, much of my vacation time from work was spent at their weekend parties and rehearsals and weddings. But that was okay; this is a natural part of life. And I believe our greatest happiness can be a result of being happy for other people. Being as excited about their life changes and wins and successes as our own can lead to incredible fulfillment. I never looked at my friends' weddings or their honeymoon getaways as opportunities to mope about my singleness or wish I was the one the celebrations were built around. Rather, I looked at how I could use these events as a springboard for my own adventures.

If you can couple an occasion that uplifts a friend or family member with an adventure you can cross off your bucket list, that's the perfect win-win situation.

My brother Jared's wedding took me across the Atlantic. He had told me months before that he planned to propose to the young Irish woman he'd met on a blind

"I BELIEVE
OUR GREATEST
HAPPINESS CAN
BE A RESULT
OF BEING
HAPPY FOR
OTHER PEOPLE."

date. I knew it was coming, but I couldn't contain my excitement when he announced his engagement. Not only was Sarah already a dear friend, but the wedding would be in her home country of Ireland. What a fantastic opportunity to pair an adventure in a gorgeous and historic country with the celebration of a wedding.

In addition to spending time with my family in gorgeous Irish locales, I wanted to cross another city off my bucket list: Edinburgh. After securing my plans for the wedding, I added a week in Scotland. I could decompress from both the family event and being the soloist at the wedding by spending time in a place that had long been my dream to visit. My brother's wedding plans would catapult me to Ireland, and after the ceremony, I could go further.

I had a lovely time exploring Ireland, including Cobh (pronounced *cove*), an island at the tip of Cork City's harbor on the south coast of County Cork. Stepping into Dublin, however, is an immediate trip into a bookish paradise—from following in the footsteps of James Joyce, Jonathan Swift, and Oscar Wilde to viewing the Book of Kells, an eighth-century, illustrated Gospel book, and gasping at the grandeur of the magnificent Trinity College Library. The Cliffs of Moher, I had read, could make one believe in God, and I didn't doubt it as I stood on their sunny, green-spanned height and peered down to the vast blue of the ocean. Jared's wedding day was one of the happiest days of my life, but after a week with family, it was nice to find myself alone.

I took a cheap Ryanair flight from Cork to Edinburgh and stayed at a wonderful bed-and-breakfast. Edinburgh is a fabulous location for solo exploration. Stepping onto the Royal Mile and peering into every alleyway—or *close*, as the locals call it—is a glimpse into the medieval origins of the rich architecture of the city. This trip to Scotland also took me to Glasgow and on a highland tour that included Stirling Castle and Loch Lomond. The places I was seeing had such a diverse narrative. I filled up notebooks and took hundreds of pictures. The accents and songs and stories seeped deep inside me. Scotland was a different country in contrast to Ireland, and yet there was a similar cadence to its history and rich regard for storytelling.

A few years later I learned that a friend who was also a coworker would have an art show featured in the Edinburgh Festival Fringe, and once again I planned a trip. I wanted to support her, and I hoped a familiar face from home would contribute to her experience, but her show was also a starting point for a trip that took me from Scotland through Yorkshire for research purposes. I even made a stop in Haworth, famed residence of the Brontë sisters, and then I went onward to London. I was happy to see my friend on the other side of the world and to explore a side of Edinburgh I might never have seen without her showing me her work.

Travel Because of Work

Sometimes traveling is for work. For years, I worked for a large educational publisher, and the role took me all across Canada, giving me not only the privilege of travel but also a chance to see the rest of my country. Even a weekend in snowy Thunder Bay, Ontario, afforded some cold but beautiful lakeside walks and capitalizing on the city's large immigrant population from Denmark. Finnish pancakes at the Hoito Restaurant in the downtown quarter of this far north city was always a treat. I also tried to ensure that when traveling along a coast, I stayed in an interesting place during the weekend transition between two provinces in combined weeks of meetings.

One of my favorite adventures was when work took me to Victoria, British Columbia, and that included a weekend. We had a corporate rate with a gorgeous hotel on the harbor, where I befriended a few chocolate-colored seals. I took advantage of the beautiful spring weather to explore the city aptly named for the queen whose reign inspired it. So many of the buildings were of Victorian vintage, and the main street boasted tea shops and a gorgeous bookshop that made me feel as though I had stepped into another world.

I always ensured that if I had work to do on these business trips, my laptop came with me to places overlooking the ocean, or with a view of the blossoms in bloom, or with ornate high ceilings and mahogany touches, such as in an old pub. I immersed myself in the experience so that my corporate trip wasn't made up of just stressful meetings and presentations but the makings of an interesting memory.

Don't Forget What You Can Gain Because of Locals

Maybe if you love meeting new people above all else, they're the main reason you travel to a new place. But even if that's not your dream, many locals enjoy being one reason you have a great experience.

Work often took me to the Maritime provinces of Canada, often starting in New Brunswick or Newfoundland and going on to Prince Edward Island, the province immortalized by Lucy Maud Montgomery's red-haired orphan, Anne Shirley. PEI is quite different in winter than in summer when most tourists—including me—are more likely to visit. In winter, Charlottetown is a small city rendered smaller by the lack of open establishments. Yes, it's a university town, and the students are there year-round, but it's also a province whose population quadruples during the height of the summer months.

I've found that if I visit a place off-season, it takes only a good rapport with the owner of a bed-and-breakfast or hotel to learn what museums and historic sites are open. Often, just showing a local interest can literally open doors. Once, in Sydney, Nova Scotia, at the tip of Cape Breton Island, the proprietor of a small museum offered me tea and cookies while he called his friend to come open the church manse so I could tour it.

Most potential visitors would be surprised to learn that the province houses little more than 150,000 permanent residents on an island that can basically be driven in its entirety in the course of a day. Nonetheless, if Montgomery taught readers anything, it's that the character of nature affords beauty any time of year. The historic city, where in many ways Canada first became a country, has lots of museums and historic houses to counter the popular Anne destinations.

Of course, one can sample raspberry cordial, made famous in *Anne of Green Gables*, and buy straw hats with fake red braids to look like Anne, but the more time you spend in a place and talk to the locals, the more you realize that the heart of a city often lies beyond an outsider's concept of it. The world becomes smaller and your own country even more so when you take the time to find what sparks the interest and passion of the people who live wherever you go.

Sometimes a Trip Is Even Better When a Friend Comes Along

I love traveling solo, but I also enjoy opportunities to travel with a friend—as long as she understands I still need time alone!

"How many hours do you need alone to feel human again?" my friend asked me after I'd had a long solo ramble on an early spring Saturday. She made a guess. "Two? Two and a half?"

She and I were in New York City for the weekend to see a play. Our plane had been grounded on the tarmac at Pearson Airport in Toronto for hours because of snow the evening before, and it was well after midnight on Friday when we arrived. Yet the next morning, I got up early so I could get coffee and wander the streets alone before our scheduled time for breakfast together. Later, I was back with my friend, and we had a great time, but those two hours when I carved out time for myself were happily appreciated.

After the release of my first novel, I attended a book

event in Chicago, inviting my best friend, Sonja, along for the trip. She lives on the other side of Canada, and it's always fun to meet up in an interesting city and explore it together.

Like me, Sonja likes to have time alone to explore the streets with her camera and her keen photographer's eye. My event ended, and I returned to the hotel to find she had gone off for the day. She left a note telling me where to meet her for dinner, and I had the luxury of winding through the streets of a city whose history I loved, staring up at the architecture and taking my time.

I try to choose traveling companions who recognize that I'll need my own moments, just as sometimes I need moments alone while home for family Christmas, stealing away to Starbucks for a little while to escape the noise. Wherever you land on the Enneagram or Myers-Briggs scale, carve out a little time alone to appreciate your travel experience without distraction.

A lot of adventure comes to us when we're open to the spaces and places and even locals around us. Whether you're traveling of your own idea and volition or because or with others, don't waste an opportunity to discover something new. No matter where you are in the world, from a hotel boardroom to a small-town square, there's always an interesting experience to be had.

A Word About Empathy for Others

Did you know adventures can teach us empathy for others? The savvy adventurer recognizes that no adventure is *just* about her—no matter how alone she is in its undertaking. Confidence is gained too in the attitude and approach we take with all the people we encounter.

On landing back home in Toronto after a weeklong business trip to San Diego (I'll tell you about it later), I learned that my luggage had been lost. My suitcase, filled with new business clothes, took three weeks to be returned, and I never did receive compensation, but in hindsight, I acted out a valuable lesson under that moment of frustration.

While the other travelers on my flight were visibly angry and understandably tense, I stabled my exhaustion and ironed the annoyance from my voice. I tend to steer away from conflict anyway. Yet jet lagged and bone tired from that week as a whole and suddenly being faced with returning home at two in the morning without all my belongings irked me.

But as I watched a coworker lash into the woman behind the airline counter, someone who clearly had no control over the lost luggage, I remembered I was traveling under a company name, on someone else's dime. This was my first post-college job, but I knew my behavior was a reflection of my workplace. That's not to say my first inclination would have been to follow the lead of the irate and angry travelers. But remembering who I represented was a salient reminder of what my behavior should be. And I was not going to treat the woman at the counter, who was not having a great day either, badly. I mustered some empathy for her. Nor should I ever treat anyone badly in my travels—not workers, not guides, not strangers, not companions—just because I'm tired and frustrated. They have their own fatigue and frustrations, and maybe instead I can make their day a little brighter.

*C*obh's cathedral, St. Colman's, is one of the tallest buildings in Ireland. Perhaps it's most famous, however, for its role in transporting immigrants across the Atlantic Ocean. It was the departure point for 2.5 million of the six million Irish who immigrated to North America during the devastating potato famine from 1848 to 1850. In the next century, it became well known as the final port of call before the *Titanic* set out on its ill-fated voyage in April 1912.

Expand on an Event

- Find out if any further travel deals are associated with the hotel or resort where your event is taking place.

- If your event is during an off-season for the place you want to travel to, consider that the off-season can mean reduced rates but often means fewer places are open and fewer tourists will be there. Weigh this against the comfort, accessibility, and perhaps increased safety of traveling during peak tourist points.

- Once you get to your second destination, ask the locals for their recommended activities and restaurants and make a list. If you hear any suggestions more than once, move them to the top of your list.

- If traveling with others for the first part of the trip, double up on items you can share, such as sunscreen or hairspray.

- Look into how you can inexpensively travel to another city or town from your event, perhaps by carpooling with other guests.

- A new place to visit in addition to the original trip is always fun, but perhaps consider visiting family or friends on the way home and letting that be your special second place. You may already be familiar with the sights in the city you'll be landing in, but there is nothing like connecting in person with people you love who don't live close to you. Though you may travel directly to your main event, consider letting the return trip home stop over somewhere so you can hug someone you haven't seen in a while.

- Did you bond with a bridesmaid or wish you could reunite with a second cousin you haven't seen since the last family gathering? Use the time after the event to intentionally reconnect and pursue friendship. If you are a little afraid of small talk, remember that when you are both experiencing and seeing something together for the first time, it's an immediate topic of conversation and a lifelong memory.

Part of this adventure will be spent with other people. Take a moment to compare how you experience a setting, venue, or site with others versus how you encounter it alone.

....

....

....

....

Are your senses more attuned to a collective experience and more likely to go with the flow of a group when you're traveling alone rather than when traveling with someone else? How so?

....

....

....

....

....

What are you experiencing with others that you would rather experience alone when given the opportunity? For what experiences would you appreciate having a companion? Do you think your feelings about this might change as you spend more time independently traveling?

....

....

....

....

....

....

....

....

....

....

....

....

....

....

....

CHAPTER THREE

The Inspired Adventure

I avoid looking forward or backward,
and try to keep looking upward.

CHARLOTTE BRONTË IN A LETTER TO
AUTHOR ELIZABETH GASKELL

*Y*our motivation for traveling might be to trace family history or to step into a film you've loved since childhood. Perhaps your elementary school teacher featured a unit on a place that has long resided in your mind. But I have a confession to make: The majority of my hankering after travel correlates with my lifelong love of reading. A good author and an immersive book is often the gateway for my wanting to read more about a place and finally experience it for myself.

Long after my grandmother's death when I was a toddler, I learned Vienna was her dream city. The year before Oma's death, she finally made it to *Wien*, pronounced with the harsh *v* my mom says so perfectly punctuated her native Dutch accent. A war bride from Holland, she immigrated to Canada with my grandfather, whom she met during the occupation. But she never forgot her passion for the Baroque city of the continent she left behind. The more I heard about Oma's love for Vienna, the more I wondered if I had inherited some of it. Yet I know my love of Vienna came from a book I read for the first time at the age of ten. *Vienna Prelude* by Bodie and Brock Thoene featured a romance between a violinist in the Vienna Symphony Orchestra and a brash American reporter for the *New York Times* in the years preceding World War II and Hitler's occupation of Austria.

Books are often behind a passion for a place. How many nursery rhymes are part of the fabric of our mental images of London? How many people have wanted to travel to Prince Edward Island because as children they read about Anne's adventures there? How many tourists moved New Zealand to the top of their travel list after its breathtaking landscapes unfolded before them in The Lord of the Rings? The inspired adventure is special because it's a link between a personal passion and a location. Often, it's linked to memory. There's a special connection between what possesses our imaginations in our formative years and our desire to experience those locations in "real life." Sometimes these adventures are unexpected. Often, they're off the beaten path. Always,

*"THE INSPIRED
ADVENTURE
IS SPECIAL
BECAUSE IT'S
A LINK BETWEEN
A PERSONAL
PASSION AND A
LOCATION."*

they're a conversation starter. I love hearing the reason certain places hold such mystery and inspiration to people; it's often a glimpse into their personality and tastes.

I've been fortunate. Several of the places I've been deeply inspired by have been on my travel list. As a kid, my favorite subject in school was history. Anytime we talked about Canadian history, I took notes fastidiously. I may have been a horrible math and science student, but I looked forward to history homework. Places like the old Jesuit mission of Saint Marie Among the Hurons an hour from my hometown and Toronto's first mayor William Lyon Mackenzie's house always excited me. And L.M. Montgomery—the author renowned for putting Prince Edward Island on the world map—lived more than half her life and wrote more than half her books in Ontario. In my own province, I was able to see the manses she lived in while her minister husband, Ewan, preached at a church nearby.

Of course, because I was a bookworm, my interests extended to places across the ocean with an author or a character at the helm. Baker Street in London was always high on my list, and a highlight for me was touring that address, complete with a museum that featured the sitting room Sir Conan Doyle created, occupied nearly every night by John Watson and Sherlock Holmes as they consulted on interesting cases in gas-lit Victorian London. But then there was author Charlotte Brontë.

My Brontë Experience

Not only did I want to see where Charlotte Brontë grew up in her formative years in a small Yorkshire village, Haworth, but I wanted to visit Brussels, the city where she lived and worked as a teacher and the setting for my favorite of her novels, *Villette*.

Haworth is situated amid rolling hills and shadowy clouds that sink low over the horizon and lend an eerie palette to the bales of hay and plots of grass swerving down from the gentle slope of hills. I stayed at an old farmer's inn where I imagined weary travelers would saunter to water their horses and spend the night before the last stretch to a town of markets and progress. The Haworth parsonage was known to me from years of reading Brontë lore and legend, so when I encountered its murky yellow brick and slate black shutters, I felt as if I was meeting an old friend for the first time.

I walked where Charlotte and her sisters, Emily and Anne, walked and peeked behind the curtain of their domestic life. I wandered through the adjacent cemetery, populated by uneven gravestones like crooked teeth in a gapped mouth, and I went up to the church where her parson father, Patrick Brontë, took the pulpit every week. The silence in that church was movingly chilling from the arched windows to the cold tiles. I sought out the place where Charlotte and her sisters were buried. Then I had the village to myself. As I rambled through moors and farmland and crooked, narrow streets, I wondered how the long-lasting genius we associate with the Brontë sisters could have been cultivated in such a small place.

I had lunch at a pub where their brother, Branwell, often wasted his hard-earned money, and I took pictures of signs of street names that honored the town's industry of weaving and sewing. I even encountered a field of rather friendly sheep.

Not a year later, I was in Brussels. When Charlotte Brontë went there—largely on her own independent adventure—it was the first time she'd spent on the continent and away from home. There, she taught English to mostly French-speaking students and fell in love with her married professor, Constantin Heger. She learned to be completely alone in Brussels and was most lonely in the summer months when the family she was staying with left. She was without students and with only a foreign city at her behest.

I walked the streets she walked and visited the site near the Bozar arts facility where the Pensionnat Heger, a boarding school, once resided and where Charlotte lived as a teacher. The years I spent as a teenager reading and re-reading *Villette* became a part of my experience, like a knapsack of memories I tugged along with me, reconciling what I was seeing for the first time with my preconceived ideas. I carried a copy of *Villette* with me as I visited all the known locations from the book, and my inspiration sparked alive.

Imagination vs. Reality

Something is so amazing about meeting places we've long dreamed about for the first time. Because I'm such a Victorian literature buff, I've pursued London for years. For instance, each time I return, I find myself meeting the former home of the Marshalsea Prison, home to Charles Dickens's *Little Dorrit* and several imaginative sprees of my own. While the prison itself is long gone, the walled gate across the South Bank still stands. Wandering to it takes you through the Borough Market and by Southwark Cathedral.

But places can also be a little bit different from what we imagined. Like most Canadian children, I grew up with the Canadian Broadcasting Corporation's miniseries adaptation of *Anne of Green Gables*. I've found more locations from it in and around Toronto than I did on my first trip to Prince Edward Island. Yes, Cavendish and North Rustico, the real-life counterparts of fictional Avonlea, are beautiful, but they didn't match the imagined space I had created in my head from that series. Prepare yourself for the possibility that the *real* place is not exactly what your imagination had in mind.

These inspired adventures are never the last-minute vacation deals we see on the internet. They're rarely the ones built into a trip you take because of another person. Rather, they're the ones we save for and scrimp for and cherish because we hold the source of them so close to our hearts.

Then, too, part of the wonder of seeing the world in a brilliant and new way is recognizing that you can be inspired anywhere. That includes the spiritual adventures we'll talk about in chapter 7.

*C*harlotte Brontë, best known for writing *Jane Eyre*, was one of three sisters whose works are a timeless representation of female voices in the Victorian era. Beginning in 1842, she and her sister, Emily, taught English and learned French under the tutelage of progressive teacher Constantin Heger while boarding with his wife and children. Later, Emily went back to England, leaving Charlotte on her own.

Charlotte was greatly influenced by Heger, and many scholars cite his influence in the character of Mr. Rochester in *Jane Eyre* and later as the hero Paul Emanuel in *Villette*. *Villette*, or "Little Town," is Brontë's recollection of her experiences in Brussels. When she returned home to England, she wrote her beloved teacher numerous letters, eventually not answered—a haunting reminder of an unrequited attachment.

Make Yourself Comfortable

- If you can, bring your pillow with you. Packing it in your suitcase will help everything stay in place and protect fragile items. You might also find it helps you sleep better in a strange bed, and there is nothing like a good night's sleep to make an adventure more fun.

- And speaking of pillows, a neck pillow for even a short flight or train ride can make travel so much more comfortable. It doesn't have to be bulky and a pain to carry. An inflatable neck pillow will quickly deflate at the end of your journey and fold into a small square that easily fits into a purse or pocket.

- You might prefer to mimic the routine that makes you comfortable at home. Set your alarm, determine your mealtimes, and carve out an itinerary that allows you to feel settled.

- If you've had a long overnight flight, drink caffeine and lots of water and stay awake until time for bed that evening. This will jump-start your new schedule, and the next morning will go a lot better!

- Don't be afraid to ask your hotel concierge for anything that will make your stay more comfortable. If you like your room to be at a certain temperature and can't change the thermostat yourself, call the desk and ask for help. If your room doesn't come with a luggage rack in the closet, see if you can get one delivered. Having your suitcase elevated a little makes it much easier to access during your stay.

- Tips and tricks to make your hotel stay a bit more luxurious and refreshing: Use hand towels to create a moisturizing facemask with hot water. Bring a small bottle of your favorite bubble bath to have a relaxing soak. Consider using the clips on a trouser hanger from the closet to clip shut the curtains so light leaks don't disturb your sleep.

- Does a candle, book, blanket, or photo of a family member ground you at home? You can create a temporary home wherever you are by bringing a small memento or two.

What places inspire you? What does this say about your personal tastes and preferences?

....

....

....

....

....

....

....

....

....

....

....

What movie or book formulated your first concept of a place? How does your adventure there compare to how it's represented in that book or film?

....

....

....

....

....

....

Imagine your adventure as if it were being considered for a book or movie. What unexplored corners would they choose to focus on instead of the more popular sights and sounds?

....

....

....

....

....

....

CHAPTER FOUR

The Adventure in Unexpected Meeting

I am a part of all that I have met.

ALFRED, LORD TENNYSON

I caved in Salzburg.

I was determined not to take part in the cheesy *Sound of Music* bus tour, but I had grown up with the film. And while Austrians don't understand the North American love for it (it played there for only a weekend), they appreciate the tourism. So I signed up and waited outside my hotel for a large bus with a huge Julie Andrews photo on the side to take me throughout the city and beyond to all the sights famous because of that movie.

For a long time, I thought "Edelweiss" was the Austrian national anthem, my earliest conceptualization of Austria coming from my childhood memories of *The Sound of Music*. So much of my childhood unfolded in memories of watching *The Sound of Music.* Encountering Austria in person made me reconcile my fictional ideas with reality. As I stepped onto the tour bus, I was in my own world, staring out the window and taking in the gorgeous scenery, realizing that a favorite childhood film was merely a snapshot of the glorious landscape in which it was set. Then I focused on the voices around  me. This was a tour group consisting of a demographic older than me, perhaps of retirement age. But it wasn't what I *saw* that startled me; it was what I *heard.* An accent familiar to me. A *Canadian* accent. But not just any Canadian accent. It was a distinctive dialect indigenous to the island of Newfoundland—fondly known as "The Rock." I turned with a bright smile to address several passengers at once.

"You're all from the Rock!" I said, delighted. On the other side of the world, I'd found a conclave of people from a province I absolutely adore. Sometimes when you're pursuing your own adventure you find the most unexpected meetings.

Connection can spark in many ways. Sometimes it's because of a shared experience—a laugh over a mixed-up order in the Starbucks line, picking up the wrong dry cleaning, accidentally sitting in the wrong seat at a concert. And sometimes it's a little more romantic. When an unexpected connection occurs between the hero and heroine in a movie—humorous misunderstandings that bring two people together for the first time—and leads to romance, it's called a "meet cute." And that can happen.

But I like to expand on that idea so the connections I make aren't merely defined under the umbrella of traditional romance. I believe there's a special affinity between a person and a place, which is why we recall a favorite restaurant from childhood or the smell of our piano teacher's Victorian home. And sometimes, if we're truly fortunate, we find a connection with a place *and* with a human being at the same time. Often, that kind of connection is wonderfully unexpected.

I romanticize solo travel because I enjoy it so much, and yet it's not without its moments of…reality. Women traveling alone do have to be careful when they interact with others; they must be aware. But refuse to let a fear of connecting—especially with men—deter the enjoyment of your trip as a whole.

A Word About Personal Style

Making an impression while traveling alone is as much about making you feel confident as it is how you are viewed by anyone you might encounter along the way.

The more I traveled for work and research and fun,

the more I recognized that my personal style is a means of confidence. I've always felt more confident when displaying my penchant for jewelry, red lipstick, and prints and scarves, the latter either tied around my head or my neck. My sense of fashion is very much *my* sense. I never particularly mull on it as a means to draw attention but rather as a means of being myself.

It also emboldens me to dress well. After a red-eye flight, landing for a transfer in Warsaw, a woman in the airport washroom complimented me on my lipstick and hair and wrinkle-free jumpsuit and, of course, bold leopard-print scarf. I told her my dress provided me with courage: a suit of armor. If I'll be landing in a different part of the world where I don't speak the language or know the currency or know my way around, I want to *look* like I do.

She took the pointers, not to emulate but as customizable advice. Whatever makes you feel comfortable in your own skin or powerful enough to take on a new challenge works as well for traveling as it does for a big presentation or business meeting. *Dress for the job you want,* we often hear. Dress for the experience you want too. Don't dress to attract attention but to feel as if you can take on the world. I always dress for a flight in a way that makes me feel confident. Women can do a lot with tights and a tunic and a scarf, allowing them to feel comfortable while still put together.

And that brings me to my stories.

It's Not Always About Romance

These stories take place in Paris and Vienna and Brussels, three cities I consider romantic. But they aren't about romance as much as they're about what we might want from our solo adventures.

THE PARISIENNE

Once while in Paris, I was rambling near the Palace of Justice when stopped by a gentleman in business attire—not with a wolf whistle or a proposition so much as with an interested interaction. In other circumstances, I might have made an escape, but it was broad daylight in a populated area, so I had no reservations in letting him walk with me a few blocks as he asked me questions about my style, my lipstick, and what I was doing in his city. I found it ironic to be telling a well-dressed Parisienne man in the city of fashion that everything I was wearing—except for my shoes—was secondhand. And not from some vintage boutique or high-end consignment store full of one-of-a-kind designer items but from Goodwill—even my purse.

I took a moment to assess myself: red hair and lip-stick; bright-turquoise, leopard-print scarf; bright-pink handkerchief skirt. "I love color," I told him, "and I feel more like myself when I wear it."

Many women might have found romance in this mo-ment. I'd been approached by a Frenchman who noticed my wardrobe and then wanted to take me for a long lunch and then drinks and a private tour of his Paris. But I took this unexpected meeting for what it was to me—a few moments complimentary enough to allow me to straighten my shoulders and continue to stroll along the boulevards of the famous river under a beautiful August sky, the kiosks and shops of book-sellers and painters bordered by full-blooming trees. I had an appointed time to tour the bell towers of Notre Dame, and in that moment, a date with archi-tecture was far more important to me than a date with a human being.

Not all men who approach women this way are as innocuous as this man was, but that doesn't mean women should forego opportunities for connection or not dress the way they prefer on a trip, whether stepping onto a Paris street or strolling through an airport.

THE AUSTRIAN RESCUER

I was wearing a purple top when I met Klaus, the young man I told you found me wandering, hopelessly trying to distinguish between two Viennese streets that sounded so similar. That top has long since been donated to charity, but it's been captured in selfies, revealing that I had a scarf in my hair to keep it from falling in my face in the murky July humidity.

Klaus and I had more than a connection. We had an affinity. We laughed easily together, and even as someone whose independent travel is often an escape from the pressures of small talk and forced connection, I was natural with him. He wrote his favorite spots in Vienna in my journal, and more importantly, his favorite coffee. Then his phone number.

I found my street, and he carried on his way.

I went back to my hotel and logged into one of the lobby computers, and then I emailed my aunt and close confidant, Annette, who was six hours behind. She had just seen the film *Taken* starring Liam Neeson, who played a man dealing with the abduction of his teenage daughter who'd been traveling alone. I was in my late twenties, but my aunt's daughters were not. She cited the movie when she said I should decline any further interaction with Klaus. Or at least watch my drink. But mostly, I should decline.

"That's a little dramatic," I responded. I spent the next several days enjoying the glorious sunshine and opulent buildings, wandering the grounds at Schonnbrun, stopping to hear Mozart trickle out from every alleyway and whipped-creamed-colored crevice. I took in a Strauss concert, learned the secrets of the ellipsoid-domed Karlskirche, peering over the city from behind one of its Romanesque columns, and watched a Verdi opera outside the glorious Staatsoper.

I also spent days convincing myself that I couldn't relive a conversation.

I wasn't sidetracked by Annette's concern but rather by my own limitations. The more time I spent inside my head, the more I was reticent to further the connection of that memorable time on the Ringstrasse. He had missed his stop on the trolley, and I had missed mine. We did a few loops around the Ring just talking. He had loved his time studying in Canada, just as I—bleary-eyed from an overnight flight, poor sleep, and the too-bright sun—waxed on and on about my perambulatory love for his city. A city I had not truly met yet. Not truly. Just through him.

I didn't pursue the connection. Sometimes an unexpected meeting results in a memory that warms and surrounds you, one you can take back and expound upon. I realize that an anecdote about encountering a handsome and polite man who helped me navigate his city trolley might in a romantic comedy be the "meet cute" that spirals into a romantic interlude, but my romantic interlude, perhaps, wasn't meant to include another. My Viennese honeymoon, as I called it several chapters ago, was *mine*. It was an opportunity to explore a deep love of my life—Vienna. It was a moment when I fell into the fairy tale of having the entirety of my dream placed at my disposal. My expectations were high. They still are.

I have since returned to Vienna, and I will always compare any trip there to that first trip. I had reserved it for a possible romantic honeymoon, and then I found it—independently—when I was willing to step out of my expectations and live a little. I had experienced it in daydreams, but I wanted to meet it in real life.

Still, the surfaces of Vienna's Baroque brilliance have cracks, such as reconstruction after the city was bombed in WWII. I find myself torn between wanting to step back and see just the flawless beauty and recognizing that even the most perfect things in life can have a broken history. It made me think about the expectations we have when traveling. And even though Vienna exceeded my lifelong expectations, I didn't find the love of my life and move to a chalet in the Alps. I didn't call Klaus, and Vienna didn't whirl me into an unending waltz.

"You'll meet your love," a friend told me before I left

for England for my study abroad—"A summer love with an accent." During my semester in Sussex, I didn't have the romance my friend was so sure I'd have. Nor did I end up rerouting my path to spend the rest of my days in Austria with Klaus after a meet cute and lovely connection.

As much as we want to impose expectations on something, we must recognize our limitations. Being brave in traveling doesn't always extend to being as brave as we might like to be. I wasn't ready to call Klaus, whose phone number still sits in my Moleskine journal. My friend googled the number. It's still in service.

I conjure up a few scenarios where I call him, and where he is surprisingly still single, and we find ourselves yodeling into the sunset. But perhaps Klaus wasn't meant to be the man I called for coffee across the sea. But I did steal his café— Café Mozart—as my Viennese hub for a series of Vienna-set contemporary romances I write, and I use the experience as an opportunity to be more open and engaging with others in travel.

THE BRUSSELS ENCOUNTER

I touched down in Brussels the morning of my birthday after an overnight flight during which I was way too excited to sleep. The plane ticket was the result of a fortunate coincidence. On the way back from a work trip to the Canadian Maritimes, I was offered a sizable voucher if I took a later flight. This was the solo traveler's dream! A ticket to anywhere I wanted, and I wanted to go to Brussels—not only to trace the steps of author Charlotte Brontë, but also to see the Grand-Place, the main square in Brussels, and visit the Royal Palace and the Museum of Musical Instruments.

Once there, I checked into my hotel and then, determined to find caffeine and immediately run about the city, I left.

La Grande-Place was golden in the setting of February dusk, rose-tinted for the occasion. I snapped pictures and listened to the bells as I watched couples fall into each other's arms and teenagers with selfie sticks.

"May I kiss you?" a handsome, well-dressed man asked. "For Valentine's Day?"

It sounded like something out of a movie—and I grabbed the chance amid the light and the lightheadedness of my jet lag. Why not have a moment—just a moment—of romance on the other side of the world on my birthday? The kiss was chaste and gentle yet enough to warm me and tingle my fingertips. It was pretty much a perfect moment.

But that was all it was—a *moment.*

Women who travel alone must recognize that we

can't impress the responsibility of continued connection upon moments like these. We can't read into them a future or a lifetime. But it can be reasonable and valid and healthy to enjoy innocent connection that doesn't need to follow you home.

Your solo travel should be crafted for your own enjoyment. Traveling near and far takes time and investment, and you deserve an experience to remember regardless of other people's desires. It isn't unfriendly to carve out an experience beyond the expectations of others. You're already defying expectation by being bold enough to enjoy your own company. And it's not cold or unfriendly to decline someone's invitation; it just means tweaking your experience to suit your own needs.

The Best Connections Are Forged by Smiles

Boston is one of my heart cities. I lovingly pay tribute to its influence on my life and imagination in a fictional series of historical mysteries through which I attempt to bring the world of the 1930s to life.

One day, while staying in the city, I connected with the woman who worked at the drugstore on Hanover Street when I was replenishing my dwindling supply of notebooks. I'd been trying to use a self-checkout machine, to little success, and I was on my third credit card when she came by. The more the machine chastised me in its robotic, automaton voice, the more I smiled as I fudged my way, and the more I felt ridiculously unprepared to make this four-dollar purchase.

"What did you do?" the kind be-vested worker asked.

"I dared to try to pay on a machine." I pulled out a tone that hovered between self-deprecation and sarcasm.

"This card is Canadian," she said.

"So is its card holder."

Soon she was in stitches as a small group gathered around us.

"Yes, everyone, welcome!" I said. "Watch how inept I am at purchasing these notebooks." I let my self-deprecation fly for a collected laugh. I would never see these people again, and by that evening they wouldn't even re- 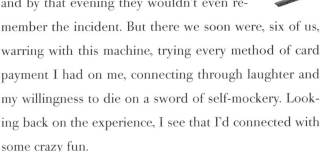 member the incident. But there we soon were, six of us, warring with this machine, trying every method of card payment I had on me, connecting through laughter and my willingness to die on a sword of self-mockery. Looking back on the experience, I see that I'd connected with some crazy fun.

Another time I wandered into the Green Dragon Tavern on historic Marshall Street, once the hotbed of revolution, after a long day of researching the historical facts I needed to conclude my trip successfully. It was around six on a sunny Friday evening, and as if peeling back the curtain of the past, several men in tricornered hats and buckled shoes, obviously finishing their day of leading walking tours on the Freedom Trail, shuffled in to watch the Red Sox play.

I straightened my shoulders and grabbed an opportunity, clutching my pen tightly, notebook open.

"If I buy your next pint, will you answer some questions for me?" I asked a man in mid-calf breeches and a vest who was also wearing a watch chain. He blended with my surroundings, as if conjured from the past. He blended with the old maps and prints and pistols. He looked at me for a moment—my pen poised, notebook open—and then accepted my proposal.

Outside stretched a world of cobblestones and the smell of bread and basil I had come to know. But inside this pub, I sipped my Diet Coke, he sipped a pint of Sam Adams, and soon the bartender and a few of his friends were fighting over the information being doled to me. I couldn't scribble fast enough as I elicited this unexpected passion for the past. These men, whose life it was to usher people into the eighteenth century, knew so much more than was probably scripted in their tours. They knew the make of the old tavern signs and about how brass items were now tinted green with age. They knew where streets used to be and where thoroughfares and development had sliced through moments of years ago.

Nothing about the exchange was untoward or hinted at their wanting to talk to a young woman alone. Rather, it was an opportunity for them to teach an outsider—a visitor—the lore and mythology of their beloved city.

The Red Sox won, and my notebook was full, but I had the sense that I was part of this community, that for that moment I belonged in this city and this history.

During my study semester in England, I met Rhonda. On multiple occasions, she and I both happened to be on the university-sponsored day trips that took us everywhere from Stonehenge to Canterbury. I truly felt a connection with her when we wandered through Lewes Castle and somehow found ourselves corridors away from the others in the group.

Without an audio tour or official tour guide, we began to weave a fictional tapestry. I roamed around manor houses and ruins listening to her commentary and adding my own insights to armor and paintings and vases. We tacked on duke and duchess and lord and lady with no actual center for the archaic and revered systems we were riffing. Seeing a carefully painted portrait, we generated a fictitious background for it. Even if we *did* know the historical background, we embellished it in our best highfalutin voices. It was innocent and a break from the intense mental power of those days.

I haven't seen or heard from her since, but whenever I think of the Duke of Norfolk or Sussex, I think of two strangers amid ancient history and tapestries flourishing a history that may...*may*...have actually happened—at least if our imaginations had anything to say about it. I'd found an unexpected kindred spirit.

When life flings you far away from what you know, you have an opportunity to find an element of unprecedented connection—and even fun. No matter how enjoyable it is to travel alone, it's in our nature to want to find connection with other humans.

In Bruges, against a backdrop of Barry Manilow tunes—"Mandy" and "I Made It Through the Rain"—I managed to find myself in the middle of another collective experience. A few Texans were working their way from England for a few continental daytrips and drives inspired by BuzzFeed articles. They were a family intent on making me feel I was a part of them, welcoming me into the sphere of their adventure and wondering if I would come along for the rest of it. I didn't accompany them, but I did laugh heartily when another family of four, from England, joined in the easy banter. You can find friends almost anywhere if you're willing to listen and engage.

Sometimes we can be the ones who initiate a connection.

Freddy

Brussels is a mélange of French and German and Dutch, but like most European cities, it also boasts a wide range of English speakers. I felt comfortable there, but for people who feel more comfortable with something they know, I recommend finding a place to return to—even a booth or table. Here, my extra comfort came from a restaurant a stone's throw from the famous old square. The broad, mahogany pillars, stained glass, large furnace, and silent films playing on screens became my nook in a touristy place that balanced just enough kitsch with history. I also ate double-cooked fries in the Belgian style with mayonnaise, which I justified with long treks all over the city.

I met Freddy at a restaurant on my first day there. He was a waiter and the first person I talked to other than a Starbucks barista at the airport and the concierge at my hotel. I took in his burgundy vest, starched white shirt, and bow tie as well as his wire-rimmed glasses and bright smile. He treated everyone as if they were the most important person ever to cross over the square and into an establishment with menus that had photographs and illustrations allowing the non-Belgian speaker to just point when they saw what they wanted.

Every time I was there, I watched him perform the careful choreography of a server with multiple stations at his command. He had a lanky grace about him and an animated face. I observed him dole out several languages, his own and others as he found a way to connect with each customer.

One evening I saw him mediate when a complaint issued in a language I couldn't decipher erupted. Freddy was summoned by two servers who didn't speak said language. In his friendly and evenly measured tone, he kept the situation from escalating. He calmly approached the table, and with the same penchant for connection and communication I'd witnessed on my first day there, he had the customers laughing in moments.

To me, this was magic. Freddy could waltz in and around tables, both inside and on the adjoining patio with a sure and winning grace. He could treat every transient customer as if they were the king or queen of England. When I travel on my own, I'm usually content enough with my journal, my thoughts, and my inspiration, but something about Freddy made me want to engage him in conversation. He loved his job. He was invested in it. He delighted in what people chose from a selection of pictures on a pick-and-point menu.

I asked Freddy to have coffee with me, in broad daylight, meeting in an easy and public meeting place. I wanted to learn more about this man who fascinated me.

Freddy and I talked about everything, including the city he loved and how he was saving money to open his own establishment. His good nature was genuine, and he was passionate about his job. For someone who wanted to work in tourism and hospitality, work that allowed him to learn and speak sev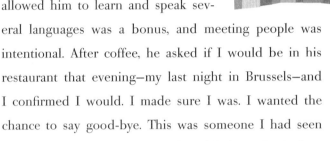eral languages was a bonus, and meeting people was intentional. After coffee, he asked if I would be in his restaurant that evening—my last night in Brussels—and I confirmed I would. I made sure I was. I wanted the chance to say good-bye. This was someone I had seen only ten times in the whole of my life but who had an impressive influence on my Brussels experience. I went back that evening and sat writing by the window.

"Will you write about me?" he asked.

Then, I didn't know. Now, I do. Yes, Freddy, I wrote about you.

Take a Chance

It's special to revel so much in a connection and be so aware and alive in its moment—with the rest of the world falling away—that you hold on to it. Moments like these are tangible souvenirs just as much as a shot glass or a postcard or a tote bag, and I've found that my happiest travels are a balance of my own company and when I open myself up to conversation, a moment, a coffee. Sometimes it's enough to take the opportunity for a conversation or meeting without Facebook friending or email exchanges or texts thereafter. Sometimes a moment is just that—a moment.

When you try to connect, you might crash and burn, or say the wrong thing, or feel like you've tripped onto your face. But part of the beauty of independent adventure is finding the courage to try and fail, the courage to be vulnerable.

*J*ust over the hills from Salzburg, high atop a steep and uneven hill in the Bavarian mountains, is Hitler's Eagle's Nest or *Kehlsteinhaus*. Hitler often vacationed in the area of Obersalzburg (direct translation: over Salzburg), but as he rose to power, he found a far more potent use for it—his Eagle's Nest. The building was completed in a record 13 months, capitalizing on the rigorous advantage taken of workers with little choice than to see its hasty construction. Because Hitler was terrified of heights, he traveled up the hill with car windows blackened, and the elevators in the building are still mirrored and brass as they were to alleviate his claustrophobia. Now a restaurant, beer garden, and tourist area, this site still bears the scars of its dark history, including grooves in the marble fireplace mantel bearing marks made with the butts of victorious American rifles.

Smart Precautions

- If you ever feel you need an extra border of protection around yourself, it's okay to adopt a cold demeanor. You can also wear headphones without music to deter anyone from approaching you.

- Use daylight hours to prepare for any sojourn at night. Also, make sure you always have a clearly available exit wherever you are.

- Note where convenience stores and restaurants are so you always have a place to duck into if you ever feel unsafe.

- Pack an extra charger so your phone battery is never dead. If you need to, however, go to hotel lobbies. They often have universal chargers available, as do international restaurant chains like the Hard Rock Café.

- Carry a small whistle and a tiny flashlight in your pocket. Besides being a possible deterrent if you feel threatened, the whistle could alert someone if you are injured and need help, while the flashlight will provide illumination in dark places. That could help you walk safely on unfamiliar surfaces at night, such as cobblestones.

- Consider wearing a fake wedding or engagement ring if you're single because not all men will take no seriously. But in many cultures, men respect the symbol of a committed relationship and will move on.

- Never feel you must follow through on a meeting you agreed to. Feeling safe takes precedence over another person's expectation.

- Let your accommodations know beforehand that you are a woman traveling alone.

- Immediately check that the door in your room has a deadbolt lock. Don't be afraid to ask for another room if you are feeling unsafe. Inconvenience is nothing compared to your feeling of safety in a new place.

- Ask a concierge or local for maps that indicate where visitors will be safest.

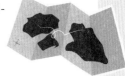

JOURNALING JUMP-STARTS

How have books and films shaped your expectations about meeting others away from home?

....

....

....

....

....

....

....

....

....

....

....

....

Can you think of a time when you met a stranger accidentally, perhaps in a grocery store or restaurant, with a unique story behind it?

....

....

....

....

....

....

Does the idea of interacting with men when traveling alone frighten you? How can you overcome that fear—responsibly and safely and without compromising any of your values?

....

....

....

....

....

....

....

CHAPTER FIVE

The Urban Adventure

A city is a place where there is no need to wait
for next week to get the answer to a question, to taste
the food of any country, to find new voices to listen
to and familiar ones to listen to again.

MARGARET MEAD

*B*ecause my dad was the pastor of the church I attended as I was growing up, I spent more time at a place of worship than a lot of kids my age. He often needed to spend some administrative time in his office after a service or take a phone call or meet with parishioners, and in the warmer months, I would wait outside on a bench and watch the cars on the highway go by. Of course, a thousand other possibilities existed, but in my head the traffic was going only *to* Toronto or returning *from* Toronto—the big city.

Sometimes that highway led me to Toronto too. I always hankered after cities. I am not sure if that was because they meant theater to me, but I always wanted to go to the theater. I thought Toronto sounded like the most wonderful place in the world because it not only had several bookstores but also blockbuster musicals and plays concurrently running with flashy marquees.

Dad sometimes took me with him on his two-hour trek to Toronto to see parishioners who'd been admitted to the hospitals there for surgery or special care. When he visited St. Michael's Hospital, he would drop me off at a  store aptly named the World's Biggest Bookstore so I could explore it. I lived for those days, and not long after, I moved to Toronto for college and stayed. Though small-town raised, I am very much a city mouse as a grown adult.

Remember that trip I took with a friend to New York City, the friend who knew I needed some time alone? I loved the opportunity to grab my journal and set out alone into the thrum of the city, passing the marquee advertising the play we'd see that night and joining the chaotic rhythm of Times Square. I stared up at the skyscrapers while my eyes adjusted to the streams of loud and pulsing fluorescence. Then I found myself in the corner of a restaurant high above the streets, the view below a splash of taxi yellow. I drank strong coffee, watched a world that rotated at a higher frequency than even my

Torontonian self was used to, and wrote.

Something in a city reminds people that they're the cog in a wheel of constant turning and industry, that things never slow down. Cities are also the perfect place to learn how to feel comfortable alone. For instance, you can be sure that no one in a large city will zone in on a solo diner, and no one in a large auditorium for a concert or lecture will think someone is out of place just because they're by themselves.

The allure of urban travel often exists because of the many plays, events, galleries, and museums, but cities also test our confidence. The city traveler recognizes that with independence comes not only an interesting perspective but also a responsibility. To those unused to the city's sounds and lights, it's imperative to share and learn from experiences, good and bad. And that's why I'll share a few stories that illustrate how travel in a big city can be challenging.

Chicago and Prague— the Taxi Experience

Chicago is a city my heart will always pursue. On one trip there, after spending time with a friend at the historic Palmer House hotel built by mogul Potter Palmer in the late nineteenth century out of love for his wife, I hailed a cab in a queue outside the hotel to return to my own hotel. I got in, and I didn't pay much attention until I realized we were driving far away from the city center, unevenly, and well beyond Lake Michigan. I started to panic, mostly because I couldn't see exactly where we were due to us leaving the center of the city's memorable skyline and lakeside buildings and street names familiar to me.

I kept telling the cab driver to turn around, but it was becoming more and more clear that he was under the influence of something. I asked him to pull over, unsure of what I would do when I got out of the cab because I didn't know where I was. I wouldn't know where to tell another cab or the police where to come. But I couldn't stay in the cab, either; his driving was becoming more and more uneven. Finally, he swerved over in the middle of nowhere and stopped.

I was terrified until I saw the flash of police lights. I got out, shaking and in tears as they arrested the man for driving under the influence. The officers were kind and had me wait by the cruiser until they found another cab for me, telling the driver they had his license to ensure he saw me to my hotel safely. This nice driver was the epitome of kindness, and when we finally arrived after a long backtrack into the city center and my hotel, he refused payment. You will often encounter good people. They are everywhere.

Every travel magazine and website I consulted warned me about the taxis in Prague. Many try to take advantage of tourists, and it's best never to hail one just off Wenceslas Square or the Christmas markets in the Old Town Square. But I had stayed out later than anticipated at the Christmas market near the Vltava River. To that point I had walked everywhere in the city—from my hotel in Dalimilova to the tourist sights and over to Malá Strana across the river—and I knew I would feel safer not walking to my hotel alone because it was on the other side of an underground train tunnel. Following the advice of so many guides, I found a chain hotel with a long taxi queue.

I knew immediately that the cab driver was not taking the fastest or most efficient route. I had spent the previous four days walking all around and had studied the maps quite extensively before my trip. I called him on it several times, but he paid no mind, looping around and around the streets as the meter shot up. I was furious, especially when he finally pulled up to my hotel and read me the charge. I bluntly told him that this was an exorbitant and ridiculous fare considering the route he took. Then I heard the doors of the car lock.

I was given an ultimatum: Either I paid what the

meter indicated, or I didn't leave the car. At that point, I knew my fighting or yelling would only make the situation worse. I didn't have the luxury of a comeback or a dismissal. I paid, dashed into the hotel, and ran up the stairs to my room.

When I tell these cab stories to people, they often question how I still find the courage to travel alone, especially in big cities. But scary things can happen anywhere in the world. No one is ever completely safe in a city or out of a city. And sometimes when you do everything right, you still find yourself in a scary situation. But that doesn't mean fear should drive your decisions or keep you from adventure. I relay these stories because I wish someone had told me their personal experiences before I ventured on solo adventures. What's more, these experiences have made me more determined than ever to continue to conquer my fears.

Vienna—Resiliency Wins

I was in Vienna visiting the Christmas markets when the news of the Berlin Christmas market attack in 2016 flashed on every television in the Innerstadt, followed by projected safety measures for all European markets. As sadly seen through the injuries and deaths caused by this driver intentionally running into a group of innocent shoppers next to the Kaiser Wilhelm Memorial Church in Breitscheidplatz, markets were an easy target. That night my social media erupted with messages encouraging me to be careful, to avoid public places the next day.

I woke the next morning to sun and sparkling snow settling over the city, making it look like a ceramic ornament on a mantel. Rather than retreat, the Viennese were in the markets in droves. It was the busiest I had encountered the squares and plazas since my arrival. It was a battle of defiance. They weren't going to be frightened by what happened; they were resilient.

If you're afraid, evil wins, and it can keep you from some amazing adventures. My takeaway from these city experiences has been positive because they have prompted me to prepare even better and to share my experiences with others in hopes that they will use what I learned firsthand: that no matter how prepared you are, there is always the chance of something veering off course. Still, never exchange optimism for fear.

The urban adventure can make us feel like we're part of something—the music of the traffic and the blink of the lights—while still being independent. Oftentimes, just exploring is akin to making your own museum. You can explore the architecture and the streets and use your imagination to peel back the curtain on history, and then picture in your mind's eye how that history may have developed from its earliest years to a booming conclave of traffic and skyscrapers.

*C*hicago's nickname, the Windy City, isn't about the weather but about the long-winded politicians who established it as a hotbed of intrigue and reform. Referring to Chicago as the Windy City has more to do with the city's bid for the famous 1893 Columbian Exposition, now better known as the Chicago World's Fair and immortalized by pictures of the almost mythical White City on the harbor of Lake Michigan still visible to visitors.

During the latter part of the nineteenth century, as Chicago was becoming one of the most populous cities in the United States, it was in constant rivalry with Cincinnati. Many journalists referred to the Windy City as the hub for braggarts and boasting—referring to either politicians or journalists.

More Smart Precautions

- Research a subway system before you use it, memorizing your stop.

- Take photos of your maps in case you're without Wi-Fi or cellular service.

- Don't take out a lot of money in a public place. And if you need to go to a bank machine, go to one inside a branch (in the daytime), not to one on the street.

- Before you go out alone anywhere, let someone know where you're headed and when you expect to be back. That could be a travel companion, the hotel concierge or a desk clerk you have connected with, or a friend or family member back home. This is an easy and simple level of safety to add to your day or evening, whether it's a hike in the woods or a night at the theater.

- Learn from people's experiences before you go, either by talking with friends or family who have visited where you're going or by searching reviews online.

- Be aware of what and where you post on social media. Some countries have strict overseers who monitor content posted on those sites. Plan to be more careful than usual in expressing your response to places and experiences.

- Take a photo of the license plate of an Uber or cab you get into so that you can send it to the police for tracking or to report someone. (Often Ubers are safer because you can track them with your location services on your cell phone and can send screenshots of those live maps to friends, family members, and even the police.)

- If you're traveling on public transit, try to sit beside an older woman. In many cultures, they're treated with respect.

- If you're considering being out after dark to see the city in a different light, look into group walking tours that will take you to some sights well in the safety of other people.

What intimidates you about exploring a large metropolis alone?
How can you prepare for and combat some of those challenges?

....

....

....

Movies and television shows often glamorize city life. From your
time in an urban adventure, what are some of the appeals of a
hectic place? Why do you think people have always gravitated to
cities such as London and New York?

....

....

....

....

....

....

Can you understand feeling alone even in the midst of several people?

....

....

....

....

....

What challenges keep people from cities in today's climate? How can conquering fear enrich a travel experience?

....

....

....

....

....

....

....

....

CHAPTER SIX

————

The Backyard Adventure

We shall not cease from exploration,
and the end of all our exploring will be to
arrive where we started and know the
place for the first time.

T.S. ELIOT

*I*s this your first time here?"

A man had stopped to speak to me at Queens Quay, a main street in the harbor front neighborhood of Toronto. It was a chilly November night with a full harvest moon above Lake Ontario, which shimmered like glass. I was standing on the dock, back to the lake, looking up over the million winking lights of my city's skyline; the CN Tower, a needle piercing the sky; and dozens of condo and business buildings rimming the water. I was focusing my phone camera, and I was excited to choose a filter that would capture the rays of spliced light.

"No. I live here." I smiled with a short laugh. "I just

never quite get over it." The stranger followed my sight-
line, and I suppose he was trying to see the scene he
probably encountered every day of his life the way I was.

One of my delights is finding new places to explore in the place I live and carving out corners just
for me. Toronto is a patchwork quilt of neighborhoods.
Frequently named the most multicultural city in the
world, it's a mosaic of diversity and culture reflected
in its neighborhoods. From historic old Cabbagetown,
with the largest area of preserved Victorian houses
in North America, to Kensington Market, just east of
Chinatown and featuring foods and wares from all corners of the world, the city is a blend of culture and color
and history. I love the clash of old buildings with new,
the identifiable streetcars rumbling over the tracks and
piercing through the thoroughfare on busy Yonge and
King streets like knives.

I often take a book out to High Park, a large sprawl of
green interrupting the urban span, or wander through it
during cherry blossom season, stopping at the large lake,
forgetting that beyond the thrush of trees is a thriving
city. I love to visit Riverdale Farm, a Victorian era farm
in the middle of the city where workers steal away from
their offices to visit goats and lambs on their lunchbreaks.

But perhaps my favorite hideaway in my city are
the double-decker—stacked theaters. Built in 1913, the

building is now the last surviving double-decker theater in the world. On the bottom level is the glorious Elgin Theatre, gilded and gold with a large proscenium arch stage lit by luminous chandeliers and several stories. Atop sits the inimitable, seven-story Winter Garden. This theater was created to give Torontonians who couldn't escape the long, brutal Canadian winters the experience of entering a garden. The scrim and curtain are a blue and green palette affording a lovely pastoral scene. From the beech leaves and lanterns dripping from the ceiling to the hand-painted garden scenes on the walls and an embellished moon, the entire auditorium evokes the feeling of disappearing into a canvas.

Sometimes I sign up for the public tour on Saturday mornings just for the opportunity to disappear and lose myself in the space. Then I walk a few blocks south to the equally Edwardian and grand King Edward Hotel and order tea and sit under a grand, large, lifelike portrait of the eponymous king. No one in the world knows who I am when I'm on these little trips in my own home city. I blend into a crowd of tourists and visitors, and sometimes I pretend I'm an important businesswoman or dignitary, imagining a scenario that would see me sipping tea at a high-end hotel or as a historian commissioned to appraise the grandeur of the Vaudeville-era theater wedged next to a pub and a Tim Hortons and a Payless. Time peels away, and I imagine. I live in a constant urban adventure that costs nothing to undertake.

For moments—just in my mind—I'm not that different from my two tiny nieces who are often princesses or veterinarians or butterflies. Alone, I entertain scenarios that never leave my mind, I daydream, and I take in the inexpensive or free beauty around me. A woman need not mortgage her house to live extravagantly. Rather, she needs only to have an open mind that allows for temporary escape. Often, the hours spent in make-believe in childhood dissolve or are replaced by watching the same penchant in children or grandchildren or nieces and nephews.

What better way to reclaim a little bit of that creative spirit than in the secrets and chapters that unfurl with the tiniest bit of effort to navigate your own hometown. An appreciation of the place where life has landed us is a gift. I guarantee you can dream and dare and adventure exactly where you are. For instance, if an old house or hotel in your town or city has always impressed you, go learn its story. Imagine that you're seeing your town or city for the first time as a tourist. How can that mind-set inform how you see what you might take for granted every day?

Your Backyard Is Bigger Than You Think

It rarely shocks city people when I tell them I don't have a driver's license. Not many people in the city do because parking is so expensive, and public transit is the faster and easier way to navigate. The one limitation is when I want a backyard adventure for a day trip nearby, especially to smaller towns with fantastic summer theater. In the past several years, coach buses have provided an opportunity for city dwellers like me to join a group in a day trip. The bus often leaves Union Station or another popular and easily accessible hub in the city and allows the attendees to choose a few different times to return.

Sometimes your backyard adventure can happen while visiting a family or friend. I love to find interesting places to visit when I'm in London, Ontario, for a weekend or holiday stay with my aunt and uncle. Downtown London hosts many yellow-bricked houses, churches, and buildings showcasing its history as a center of education and industry. It has large, sprawling parks and rivers, and the summer months are an eruption of green. Like so many other Canadian cities, London hosts a Covent Garden market in the heart of the city. I remember the first time I wandered through it, taking in the shops and counters, the greenery and café tables that lent it the atmosphere of a garden.

Niagara-on-the-Lake, Ontario, offers a view of neighboring America and none of the tourist traps and haunted houses of nearby Niagara Falls. As you're strolling down the main street—taking in the manicured lawns, the sound of a horse and buggy clopping along—you can see tourists on the way to a matinee performance at the George Bernard Shaw Festival and red Victorian buildings. No wonder part of the redemptive scene in the movie *It's A Wonderful Life*, when George Bailey yells out his love for Bedford Falls, was filmed there. It's idyllic. And it's a perfect place to retreat into tiny shops with homemade jam and cheese or to pick up the elusive knickknack or fragrance you need for a friend's birthday gift.

The Cottage at Lake Huron

"We have wine and we have books," my aunt Annette emailed me, knowing that would be enough to capture my attention. She and her friend had rented a cottage on Lake Huron (a perfectly picturesque part of Ontario), and I was invited for the long weekend. I packed my own books and anticipated long nights of conversation as blue Lake Huron lapped against wavy sand and the stars that specked a navy sky forever blue in its expanse drifted miles and miles back from the horizon.

My aunt's friend, Laurie, was an elementary school

librarian. I had met her on one occasion before, and I'd fallen into the musical lure of her voice. She was the consummate storyteller, finding meaning and theme in everything from Scholastic Book Fair selections to Dan Brown's latest bestseller. Her conversation inspired me to turn on my brain and elevate my thinking as we sat outside the rented cottage, partaking in platters of cheese and bread and hummus on the sloping lawn as the humid air coasted up from the lake. One night we listened to the thunder blast against the quell of lightning in one of those summer storms best met by candlelight, with curious peers out the window.

We indulged at a restaurant reborn from a yellow-bricked Victorian house in Goderich, a mainstay of Ontario history, and we pursued seeing the sunset twice, as per the town's mythology. We walked through streets that look a lot like Stars Hollow from the television show *Gilmore Girls*, complete with gazebo and town square. The welcome sign in Goderich includes a quote from Queen Elizabeth II, who deemed it "The Prettiest Town in Canada."

The movie theater showed only two films at a time, and that weekend *Eat, Pray, Love* was one of them. We bought our tickets. Laurie had loved the book, and I had just returned from a solo Austria-Germany trip that found me encountering so many dreams in real life. I left the film wishing I had the huge publishing advance that allowed Elizabeth Gilbert of the eponymous story to travel so long and so broadly. What I would give to spend months sinking into a place and making it my own, becoming a regular at a corner grocery store or a familiar face in the metro.

I enjoyed that weekend. I took my beach towel and a book and found a spot alone along the miles of sandy beach. I could wade into the lake and not find deep water for long stretches. I had companions, sure, but in a space where I felt comfortable enough to carve out moments alone.

The Blue Castle

In *The Blue Castle* by L.M. Montgomery, Canadian heroine Valancy Stirling lives a monotonous and repressive life in her mother's house as a 29-year-old "old maid." She escapes by dreaming of an opulent castle in Spain modeled after the Alhambra in Granada. In her imagination, Valancy is a queen admired by suitors, and she's wealthy beyond the meager means of her existence in her small Muskoka village. When she receives a letter from her doctor informing her that she has only a year to live, she throws caution to the wind and begins saying and doing whatever she pleases, finding an unexpected and lovely romance with a man who owns an island in the gorgeous Muskoka lake country. It turns out the "blue castle" of her dreams wasn't in the faraway hills of Spain but about 20 minutes from her.

Small Orillia, where I grew up, rests at the cusp of Muskoka, which is Ontario's postcard-picturesque Cottage Country. In Canada, what would be known Stateside as Adirondack chairs are more traditionally known as Muskoka chairs because they conjure the spirit of relaxation found amid craggy, rock-bordered lakes, majestic pine trees, and rustic waterside cottages—not to mention the loons, geese, beavers, moose, and all manner of wildlife (and even mosquitoes) associated with traditional Canadian landscapes.

My dad's first cousin and her husband own a cottage on Turtle Lake in Muskoka. The drive there through winding rocky roads is about 45 minutes from Orillia. I have no memories of visiting amusement parks or going on family camping trips from childhood, but I can map the interior of that cottage—and most importantly its exterior—with my mind's eye. For most of my life, the word *summer* conjured the sights and smells and stories of that lake in Muskoka.

When I was in high school, I learned that *The Blue Castle* was imaginatively set in Bala, Muskoka, author Montgomery so inspired by another lakeside town not too far from the cottage of my childhood. Indeed, reading *The Blue Castle* was like slipping into a fictional snapshot of the summer geography I had committed to heart's memory. I recognized the smell and feel and sounds thanks to Montgomery's descriptive prose. Together, the author, who beautifully captured the canvas of my near-backyard experiences and childhood, and I, a teenage sojourner, melded a mental landscape. The book created a pang of nostalgia for my childhood even though, in retrospect, my first long love affair with it happened when I was a teenager. But my sense of romance in nature was heightened, and through Montgomery's words I was revisiting a place and even seeing some of its visual poetry for the first time.

Roselawn Inn

In my last year of high school, I spent two nights alone at the Roselawn Inn, where Montgomery stayed when she fell in love with Bala and began to craft *The Blue Castle* in her mind. My mom drove me through the same winding rocky roads that spirited us to the family cottage on so many summer days. This time, though, I would experience it without family or friends. I was 18 and excited and nervous about spending two nights of a weekend by myself. I packed notebooks, pens, books, my CD player, a few favorite CDs, and my camera.

When the kind lady and gentleman who ran the inn and its neighboring museum asked if I wanted a television in my room, I declined. I was going to spend two days just reading and thinking, writing in my journal, and drinking in the place where a favorite author had spent memorable summer vacations. I ate meals in restaurants by myself, I visited the tiny library, and I sat and overlooked the waterfalls. I peered through the curtains of pines rimming the water to try to pinpoint the island where the hero in the book lives his solitary life.

Wanderlust can take us back to places we know with the intention of discovering them in a new light and with a new perspective and openness that perhaps the years have shaved away.

Next Chapters

Not long after my Bala adventure, I moved to Toronto for college. Then in between undergraduate and postgraduate studies, I returned home for just over half a year to work at a little bookshop and decide the next step in my life.

Returning to my hometown after having lived away

for five influential years was not unlike seeing it for the first time. This time, though, away from the pressures of high school and clubs and a part-time job at the mall, I got to know a different set of people: artists and authors and historians. And with their guidance, and with the maturity of a young woman, I tried new restaurants that 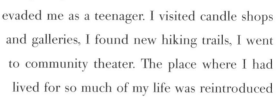 evaded me as a teenager. I visited candle shops and galleries, I found new hiking trails, I went to community theater. The place where I had lived for so much of my life was reintroduced to me at a different period in my life, when my current focus allowed me to see it with a new perspective.

Now, though I have lived in Toronto again for over a decade, I'm still baffled at the new perspectives I see of a city with corners I have yet to turn and discover. Instead of weekends that spirit me away to other cities or places, I intentionally explore a neighborhood I've never visited or taste test something new from a food truck during the summer's rotating schedule. And just as I replied to a reader, who in a message mentioned how my Toronto-set historical fiction inspired her to spend a little more time touring the city, I say, "Look up." So much of our time is spent looking at our shoes or our phones, but many of the greatest architectural treasures are known for their attention to detailing—scaffolding and window ledges, carved and etched ornamentation.

Sometimes we open the next chapter in our life's book and find ourselves on the other side of the world. But sometimes the next chapter allows us the gift of turning back a few pages and rediscovering something new in the words of our life. It requires only an adventurous spirit and an openness to revisit the places that inform who we are today.

Don't Wait

So often we associate vacation and travel with faraway places. But how often does that limit us from experiencing the adventure in our own backyard—without waiting for the means or opportunity? With so much of our lives in the place we live revolving around work and routine, we can easily do ourselves a disservice by not experiencing the places near our homes.

We can take in a local theater production, visit the farmer's market with live music, or check out a summer art crawl or a gelato stand. Our cities and towns often have local coffee shops and restaurants that would appreciate new patronage. Being a tourist in your city or town—or somewhere close by—can be a rewarding way to experience where you live with a mindful intention to separate it from the hectic pace of the workweek.

Or look for bus trips and day tours to nearby cities,

markets, or small towns you'd like to revisit. Even during a particularly busy season in life, you can find adventure. The opportunity to explore can be found wherever you are.

HISTORICAL SNAPSHOT

L.M. Montgomery, though largely associated with Prince Edward Island thanks to her beloved orphan Anne in *Anne of Green Gables*, spent most of her life and wrote most of her books in rural Ontario. *The Blue Castle* is the only one of her novels set entirely outside of PEI.

Efficient Packing

- Whether traveling in your backyard or beyond, pack only a carry-on to save on luggage fees, not to mention the perk of traveling more lightly.

- Laundry detergent pods are a great extra to pack. If you're gone for an extended period of time, you can find a laundromat and already have what you need to wash a load.

- Line your luggage with dryer softening sheets or a lavender pouch to make clothes that have been sitting in a suitcase for a long time smell fresh.

- Don't bother packing a travel iron. If you need to de-wrinkle an outfit with no iron available, hang it up while you take a hot shower and take advantage of the steam.

- Pack binder clips. They're handy for creating a place to hang up wet clothes and bathing suits over a shower rod in a hotel.

- Check Pinterest to view examples of a *capsule* wardrobe. Then pack as many outfits as possible from only a few items of clothing.

- Pack larger plastic zip bags. They can store a wet umbrella or a muddy pair of shoes.

- Take a bulky sweater or coat on the plane with you rather than packing it. Not only will this leave more space in your luggage, but planes can be chilly and those items can double as a blanket or even pillow.

- If you take a prescription medication, pack an extra week's supply in case you're stuck somewhere.

- Pack items that might not be readily available where you're going—perhaps even in your hotel or in an Airbnb—such as a small sewing kit or shoe polish.

- Extra clothes, shoes, and items can cause the fear of forgetting something behind. Plan a list that carefully allows you to use things more than once.

A Classic Capsule Wardrobe

button down shirt

long sleeve tee

simple tee

patterned blouse

colorful cardigan

pullover sweater

blazer

black skirt

dark denim

classic shift

wrap dress

ankle pants

hat

sunglasses

patterned scarf

watch

stylish sneakers

ankle boots

pointed flats

patterned clutch

leather tote

Countless Combinations

JOURNALING JUMP-STARTS

What did you associate with the word *vacation* when you were a child?

....

....

....

....

If you're visiting a place once familiar to you, what has changed since you were last there?

....

....

....

....

....

....

If you're adventuring in your own town, pretend you're a tourist. What would you recommend a visitor do? Have you done those things yourself?

....

....

....

....

....

Look up an old friend or acquaintance or visit a bakery or shop where you clearly remember an interaction with the owner or a worker. What stories have changed? Record how you may have made someone's day better by sharing the memory of your experience.

....

....

....

....

....

CHAPTER 7

The Spiritual Adventure

What we are looking for is what is looking.

ST. FRANCIS OF ASSISI

Sometimes when I hear the word *spirituality*, I think of one of those vague lines with some kind of spiritual reference uttered by a weepy Academy Award winner between thanking their castmates and producer. What they say doesn't seem to hold on to anything solid, and (as my friend would say) they sound a little "woo-woo." But at its core, the word *spirituality* refers to a person's deepest values and meanings.

For religious people, their deepest values and meanings are aligned with their belief in a higher power. And whether or not one subscribes to religion, all humans are driven by a set of ethics, meanings, and values with which they try to live their lives. A spiritual adventure, then, is a great way to reflect on what you believe and why—in a few stolen hours in a coffee shop with a book or a journal or perhaps in pursuit of a place or building that symbolizes your values and meaning. From grand cathedrals designed to draw the heavens closer to earth, in a celestial Mozart chord or the vibrant brush-sweep of a Rembrandt painting, it's always exciting to find deeper meaning and purpose in travel and to see how spirituality informs some of the greatest art and architecture in the world.

Whether, then, your spiritual adventure is inspired by pursuit of your own deeper values and meanings or a desire to learn about how other cultures and communities practice spirituality, it's a great jump-start for independent adventure. And either way, you can be mindful of reevaluating your own meanings and values as you experience a new place that allows you the time and peace necessary to do so.

I experienced a chill when I first crossed the threshold of the Eagle and Child pub in Oxford, England, knowing that around one of its stained, scratched tables, C.S. Lewis, Tolkien, and Dorothy L. Sayers spoke of symbolism and allegory, theology and the Bible. In Rouen, France, the sunset lights the ancient tower where Joan of Arc was held captive after proclaiming she'd heard God. On Edinburgh's High Street, clergyman John Knox's reputed home stands as a humble interruption among merchants and shops, and I strolled in with awe. In Fishamble Street, home to

Messiah's first performance in Dublin, I was brought to tears imagining how Handel's glorious score set to some of the Bible's most profound passages must have fallen on the ears of those who first experienced it.

In Vienna (again) at Christmas, I purchased a standing-room stall ticket to a performance of *Messiah* in the Goldener Saal (Golden Room) of the Musikverein. While the orchestra and soloists heralded Christ's birth within the Scripture-infused majesty of Handel's piece, my eyes roamed over the gold columns and up to the opulent painted ceiling, a study in perfect turquoise flourish, a rich, gilded garden. God is in music, sure, but also in structures like this.

The Majesty of Churches

In London, near St. Bartholomew's Hospital and not a far walk from Barbican tube station, St. Bartholomew the Great church is tucked away down an alley and beyond the Gatehouse, one of the oldest structures in London. Behind this grand church, William Wallace of *Braveheart* fame was executed in 1305. My romantic heart loved the popularized movie version of his tale—highlighting a man who would battle for the honor of his deceased wife and the freedom of his country. I snapped pictures of the plaque commemorating the Wallace connection and marveled at the exterior of the Gatehouse. If I shut off the world around me, I could almost imagine I was stepping centuries behind.

But not until I entered the church was I overcome with an emotion that transcended jet lag and the uncommon heat blasting from the cloudless summer sky. Something in the gravitas of the church's history—worn gravestones with names nearly completely scrubbed out underfoot and sunlight winking through the stained glass window overhead—filled me with a sense of awe. Sure, the world held many grander cathedrals, promenading with towering steeples and celestial rooftops. But in this moment, in this tucked-away church, I was still. No one else was around. It was just me and a silence from God as I inched from nave to transept.

St. James Garlickhythe church in London is known as Wren's Lantern. Architect Christopher Wren was commissioned to rebuild many of the desecrated churches after the Great Fire of London in 1666. His tireless campaign resulted in some of the most beautiful churches in the world, including St. Paul's and St. Mary-le-Bow and many of the structures immortalized in the nursery rhyme "Oranges and Lemons." Architects like Wren didn't paint or compose; they erected. Their artistry drew the eye to God. Christopher Wren had quite a hold on me.

London's St. Stephen Walbrook church has a sanctuary that leads up to the focal point of a pierced bird's eye window through an ornate stone dome. It's a mainstay of Byzantine architecture. The architectural term is *oculus*, but the French is *oueil de bouef*, or bull's eye. Craning my neck and stretching up to see the sky, my peripheral vision caught the carefully crafted sculpture of the church.

The architect and design of these churches is made resplendent by the careful constructs that allow for natural light, for God's eye to peer down from the small windows in a ceiling, mimicking scraping the sky and ascending to the heavens. Much of church design, from the arches of the windows to the steeples and spires, was crafted with a determination to lead a looker's view upward toward God.

For architects like Wren, their art and design, their brick and mortar and glass and windows, were a form of worship. An artistic expression, certainly, but also an opportunity to sow divine symbol and meaning into brilliant structures.

Churches are at the hub of a community and the heart of a newly settled place. In Sydney, Nova Scotia, the oldest churches bear the evidence of wood and metal. The immigrants from Scotland (hence the Latin translation New Scotland), assured that after they erected shelter in their new land, they began construction on the center of their spiritual and cultural lives: the church.

Knowing they would never cross back over the Atlantic to the home they'd left, they used every part of the ship that bore them to construct their first churches. No plank or nail went unused in this repurposing.

I encourage travelers to find the oldest church when they're in a new place, because places of worship are the surest way to find the natural museum of that place's history. Churches are at the center of almost every location in the world, from the grand cathedrals of Barcelona to the small wood-slatted structures that slope down to color Quidi Vidi in Newfoundland. Moreover, they don't require payment to visit. One can wander in off the street on most weekdays to be given firsthand access to beautiful architecture, stained glass, and the beauty of silence.

One need not travel specifically to find spiritual resonance, but it's wonderful to incorporate it in a trip and sew it into the fabric of your experience. A few years ago, in Boston and capitalizing on the extra days of a long Easter weekend for research, I attended the Sunday service at the Old North Church. This church is famed for the lanterns swinging in its high bell tower denoting *one if by land, two if by sea* before patriot Paul Revere set off on his momentous ride. I visit this church every time I'm in Boston, but on this specific trip I took time to explore it beyond its famed sanctuary. I descended into the crypt and ascended up to the towers and learned the narrative in its brick and stone. The reverence I held for the building and its history—both deep and abiding—paled against the significance of sharing one of the eighteenth-century vintage pews with a few strangers and following a deeply meaningful order of service.

Stepping Outside Your Own Culture and Traditions

The places I've shared align with my own religious culture and tradition. But if our independent adventures take us to different communities and cultures, the practice of religion and the meanings and values of spirituality essential to that area might differ from our own.

In Abu Dhabi, I donned an abaya, a long robe, and crossed the slick tile into the Sheikh Zayed Grand Mosque, awed by the reverence and respect surrounding the tiles, carpets, and chandeliers. The historic beauty touched even a nonbeliever and aided in my understanding of a culture so different from my own.

In the Old Jewish Cemetery in Prague, I learned about the sixteenth-century rabbi Judah Loew ben Bezalel and the Legend of the Golem, an anthropomorphic being said to have been created by the rabbi from clay to protect Czech Jews from pogroms and anti-Semitic attacks. Visitors still light candles and pray over the deceased rabbi. During my visit, a solemn silence fell over crooked gravestones, worn by years, their markings almost indistinguishable through time and wear.

The Beauty of Silence

In these moments, we can revel in silence. Our daily lives are often filled with noise, from the internet pop-up because we forgot to mute our laptops, from a neighbor's car alarm, from a yippy dog, or from a tenant who thinks blasting music will provide enjoyment for the entire apartment building. As an independent adventurer, I am often drawn to monasteries or empty churches, enclosed stone crypts where silence is revered.

In these places, you might be meeting yourself at a different stage of life or for the first time, and it's wonderful if you can hear yourself think while doing so. But if you shut off the world, the spiritual adventure should take you out of the bustle and noise and frenetic pace of your daily routine and encourage you to spend time thinking about what you believe and why—away from your Sunday morning routine or your allotted children's church duty or the new faith-based film to which you and 20 of your friends had a group discount. It need not be as grand as some of the adventures I've mentioned here, though. It may not even require your leaving town.

Last winter at a theater here in Toronto, I saw the Martin Scorsese film *Silence*, which is based on a novel featuring two missionaries in Japan during a brutal era of persecution in the seventeenth century. I wanted to not only experience it but also have time afterward to think and reflect without having to verbalize my opinion to someone attending with me. A matinee followed by a lakeside walk and a cup of tea gave me time to reflect not only on the film and its theological tenets but also on why it was important for me to see the film and how it encouraged me to think about my own values and meanings.

To you, this kind of experience might look like a hike in a nearby forest with a Bible tucked under your arm. Or sitting in the back of a chapel turned coffee shop where there's a table under stained glass that will light the pages of your blank journal. But no matter where you find it, a spiritual adventure should allow for mindfulness. And yes, for silence.

On Further Reflection

Remember the weekend I spent on Lake Huron at a cottage with my aunt and her friend Laurie—a backyard adventure? That particular weekend stands out not because I had times alone but because I also reflected on how wonderful it is to travel alone.

Sipping wine over lit candles and looking over a lake with ribbons of moonlight, I verbally asserted to my companions what has since become my mantra: Every woman needs to travel alone at least once to find out who she truly is. And because we'd just seen the film *Eat, Pray, Love*, I added, "With or without Julia Roberts's looks and author Elizabeth Gilbert's large publishing advance."

I believed that then, as I do now, because I have experienced it. For every hiccup and uncertainty in life, there is the moment of stepping off a plane in a new place, tired but excited. For every scrimped and saved penny, there is the memory of capturing the still of a castle or estate under sunlight, your brain preserving an instant in a way a camera's focus never could.

Yet alone in my room at that rented cottage, as the breeze ruffled through the secondhand curtains, I refined my mantra from earlier in the evening: A woman doesn't have to traipse across the globe to enjoy being alone. There is so much to engage in and learn and love when confronted with your own company. Perhaps even in silent, spiritual moments with meaning heightened.

HISTORICAL SNAPSHOT

*D*uring the Second World War, many of the great European churches were damaged by bombing, especially in England during the rampage of the Blitz. World War II–era footage and photographs show the smoke, debris, and calamity all around Canterbury Cathedral, in its medieval splendor, and famed architect Christopher Wren's St. Paul's, resurrected after the Great Fire of London in 1666. But miraculously, they both survived.

Before You Go

- Check your country's embassy website, making sure you know where the one in the place you're visiting is. Keep the contact information nearby at all times. Also, let that embassy know where you're going and when you'll be there.

- Research to learn about any words or gestures that could be considered offensive where you're going. Being a respectful global citizen includes learning how a culture differs from yours.

- I make it a point to learn phrases and words that will see me through even predominantly English conversations. I suggest learning "Hello," "Goodbye," "Please," "Thank you," and "Do you speak English?" in the official language of the country you are traveling to.

- Entrust a family member or friend with a copy of your passport and your entire travel itinerary. Include flight and hotel details.

- Consider any mementoes you may want to bring back with you. Make sure you have enough room in your luggage for that special something you'll see while you're away, or, if possible, bring an empty bag with you that you can use.

- Some places in the world, such as the United Arab Emirates (UAE), require a notary-signed document for permission to take pharmaceuticals across their border. Make sure you have researched enough to take care of this if needed.

- Want to take a day trip to an interesting location near where you are staying? Consider planning a bus tour via a travel site such as Expedia. This will ensure that you have cost-effective transportation to and from your port of stay as well as predetermined pickup and drop-off points. Most tour guides will arrange pick-up and drop-off times so that you can wander away from the group and experience the city or town at your own pace.

When visiting an old church, whether in your own backyard or far away, notice the names and dates on plaques or gravestones inside the sanctuary or in its graveyard. What do they tell you?

....

....

....

....

....

....

....

....

....

....

....

Initially, stained glass windows were a way to help illiterate church-goers understand and associate with well-known stories in Scripture. What motifs and vignettes do you see in churches you visit?

....

....

....

....

....

....

....

....

....

....

....

....

....

....

CHAPTER 8

The Unplanned Adventure

*Every day has the potential to be the
greatest day of your life.*

LIN-MANUEL MIRANDA

*S*ometimes the best trips are inspired by your willingness to embrace an unplanned adventure.

The first week of my (former) corporate job sent me
to California for a week of product training. In the dead
of night on New Year's Day, I took a company-paid cab to
the airport to fly to San Diego. When a stopover in San
Francisco led to a long delay, I panicked. My first day
on the job, with arrival in the evening for a social event
expected, and there I was, stuck.

I wanted so much to be the professional who met the
world she was stepping into. I had traded the cardigans
and corduroys of my university days for new business
clothes and the formal attire outlined in the company
memo. I felt like a grown-up—but a scared grown-up,

planted in an airport with only a company laptop. I wandered around. I waited. I called my new manager to no avail. Fortunately, I found a few coworkers by observing other travelers with similar corporate-issued laptops, and I swallowed my pride and approached them. But I also internalized these circumstances and felt bad, worried, and inadequate. This was a trip booked by my company's human resources department on their schedule, and I was a prisoner to circumstance.

I finally arrived in San Diego, exhausted. Starting a new job after a missed flight, feeling frazzled and uneven, was an experience I wouldn't wish on anyone. On top of that, sessions and meetings were held in closed hotel conference rooms, stifling and windowless. Meals were large events with a crippling number of people lining up in a buffet line, and, of course, the cocktail parties and dinners featured a sea of strangers.

I was so glad I had packed a favorite book and my journal to stay grounded. But I also decided I had to steal away for some adventures on my own—to try some Mexican food, to seek out the famous harbor, to shop for a bag as a souvenir of my first trip for a post-college job. None of these forays were planned beyond what my conference schedule allowed, but because I was overwhelmed by crowds and the presentation of so much new information, those outings remain a high point of that challenging week.

Often travel puts us in positions outside of our control, but sometimes an unplanned adventure helps. Then again, not every unplanned adventure comes out of a challenging experience. Sometimes they're just a delight.

Notre Dame Side Trip

I hadn't planned on tacking Paris onto a trip to England, but I had never spent time at Notre Dame cathedral. So, when I saw an advertisement on Expedia for a day trip from London, I jumped at the chance. The Eurostar train left early in the morning from London's St. Pancras station and arrived later that morning at Gard du Nord station in Paris. While the rest of the organized group set off for a boat cruise and lunch, I informed the tour leader of my solo plans and hopped on the metro to St. Michel station. Later, on the day the cathedral burned in April 2019, I compared what I was seeing on my TV screen with my amazing memories of first seeing the church towering over the Seine.

Its distinctive front flanked by those beautiful bell towers and drawing the eye up to the round Rose window is how most people conjure the cathedral's façade in their head. But surrounded by trees and bordered by the rimming Seine, Notre Dame is a grand and spacious building far larger than one might imagine from photographs.

The sanctuary and ground floor are open to the public, and the lines on that beautiful August day were long. But I took pictures of couples in line who saw the advantage of meeting a single traveler. (I never mind these requests; you can build your confidence as a solo traveler by even *offering* to take pictures of others and maybe helping them when you've figured out something they might not know.) I also practiced my limited Italian and high school French as the line crawled along.

After I explored the main part of the cathedral, I collected a time when I could come back to line up again, this time for a visit up the bell towers to take in the view of the city from above. I had several hours to stroll the Seine and stop to gape at architecture, to eat cheese and a baguette at a café, and to squint and try to imagine the city as it was when it was the cultural center of Europe. I stopped numerous times to turn my head over my shoulder and see that Notre Dame was still there. Its bells followed me as I walked.

Later that night, I hopped back on the Tube in London, bound for my hotel, and thought about the whirlwind adventure I'd just had. One reason for its success was that I had a clear goal—exploring Notre Dame. Steering off that course might have resulted in my being stressed about arriving back at Gard du Nord for my return Eurostar trip.

One of the most enriching aspects of independent exploration is putting your own passions and identity into action. Your passion might not be church architecture, but perhaps seeing a piece of art like a Rembrandt or da Vinci's *Mona Lisa* could be the goal of your unplanned adventure.

St. John's Explored

I was out east for a work trip and exhausted by Friday night, but I had a full Saturday in St. John's, Newfoundland, before leaving for New Brunswick on Sunday. I contemplated sleeping in on Saturday and then spending the day lounging in my hotel with no planned adventure. But because I had been to St. John's dozens of times and always bemoaned the fact that I couldn't explore more of it due to an intensive work schedule, I immediately mapped out a wish list of places I'd like to see and things I'd like to do. On Saturday morning I went exploring.

I look at every place I visit as a potential museum without the admission price, and because I love to walk and ramble, my favorite thing to do is set out and explore on foot. Sometimes this keeps me in populated city centers, and sometimes it takes me into nature.

From the Basilica Cathedral of St. John the Baptist

to the "jelly bean" rows of wooden houses slatted and swerving from the hill in the direction of the water, I met a city I had long been familiar with—but in a new way. I saw it as a tourist, not as a temporary resident for a business trip. After taking in all the sites of the city proper, I mapped out a hike that would take me up and around Signal Hill and then out to the fishing village of Quidi Vidi. I had never been so happy to have thought ahead, bringing appropriate footwear "just in case."

Signal Hill was the location of the last battle of the Seven Years' War fought there in 1762. What was previously known as "The Lookout" became known as Signal Hill. The citadel on top of the high hill was manned against possible enemy invasion in the War of 1812 and again during the American Civil War in case of enemy approach. At the top of a winding uphill trail, one is rewarded with a lookout tower and a gorgeous view of the Atlantic. But getting to the top, especially on a windy day, takes perseverance and stamina, not to mention a hooded windbreaker. Never did I more appreciate still hearing my mom's voice from whenever I'd set out on a field trip as a student: "Layer, layer, layer." On the ascent, one minute I was attacked by gale winds, and the next minute it was a sunny, calm, unseasonably warm day for October.

One of my rewards high atop the hill was the Ladies'

Lookout, a point named for the wives and sweethearts who ascended to watch for the ships that would bear their men home from fishing, exploration, and war. Another was the sheer power of the Atlantic Ocean, the horizon so blue it momentarily blended with the sky so I couldn't distinguish where one line ended and the other began.

After taking my time in and around Signal Hill, I made my descent, the sun nearly blinding. From there, I set out on the long walk to Quidi Vidi, a picturesque fishing village outside St. John's proper. When I arrived, I encountered a craggy, uneven place with small huts and houses jutting out of sloping rock, a wooden church that might have been there for well over a century, and a brewery that boasted a restaurant. Overturned boats catching the sun and lobster traps rimming the rocks that bordered the ocean were Instagram ready. I tried to imagine stories of the people who lived here through all seasons, what the place might look like in the dead of winter or at the first hint of spring's thaw. I left with a clear memory as tangible as a postcard and a nice break from the intensity of my work trip.

As an independent traveler with a job, exhaustion after a busy week can be a deterrent—as can the extra awareness required to navigate a new place. But I always consider when I might have the opportunity to be in that place again. Often, that's enough to propel me into action.

Maybe I don't have much time for my unplanned adventure. Maybe I can visit only one museum or historic house. Maybe I can only combine an experience with a meal. But an adventure is an adventure.

Unplanned Adventures in One Day

Unplanned adventures—perhaps on a day you suddenly find yourself free of a commitment—might just take the form of a historical walking tour in your own town or finally checking out a local museum. Have you ever wondered what the sunrise looks like over the lake where you live? Why not decide on a Friday night to set your alarm for early on Saturday and check it out with coffee and a croissant? What about the new Indian restaurant that just opened downtown? Give your meal plan the night off and make a reservation for one.

If you're away from home, however—perhaps on a trip because of someone else—make sure you're healthy and ready for extra travel with the stamina you'll need to explore for hours on end. And manage expectations. It's better to choose one thing to do and do it well than to try to cram in too much. If you overshoot, you might end up anxious and stressed, which defeats the enriching opportunity of an unplanned trip.

Unplanned adventures count—and often they're much easier to take when you're on your own.

Newfoundland and Labrador sit on the most eastern coast of Canada and feature some of North America's oldest history. Water Street in St. John's, Newfoundland, the largest city in the province, is the oldest street in North America. But perhaps one of the best-known tourist hubs is L'Anse aux Meadows (or Bay of Meadows or Grasslands). In existence prior to European settlement, it bears witness to over one thousand years of history, and it's the only confirmed Viking site in North America.

More About Air Travel

- A perk of traveling alone is that airlines often need only one person to give up a seat on an overbooked flight. If they offer a voucher for a later flight, consider tweaking your schedule and using the time you'll gain by accepting the voucher to cross another place off your bucket list.

- Add an hour to suggested airport arrival times for your own peace of mind and to stay ahead of security back-ups.

- Familiarize yourself with the gate of departure as well as the layout of your airport during a transfer. Large air-ports often require shuttles or long walks through the terminal, so a perceived long wait on a layover can end up being stressful. If you are concerned about a transfer, contact your airline ahead of time so that they can help you plan accordingly.

- Prepare for the security line at the airport. For example, rather than wearing lots of jewelry or boots, leave them in your bag so you won't have to remove them. Also ensure you know the regulations about liquids and gels and have them easily accessible at the top of your carry-on in a clear bag so you can easily retrieve them. And keep all your electronics with you in an accessible case so you can easily provide them to the security agent if asked.

- Use friends and family advantages if someone you know works for an airline. But did you know, for instance, that some airlines have dress codes? Remember that you're a guest representing your friend or family member and adhere to any guidelines.

- Get to the airport with more than enough time. It's better to be there early and calmly deal with unexpectedly lengthy lines through security than to arrive at the last minute and worry you'll miss your flight.

- Familiarize yourself with the rights of each airline for air travelers. For example, if your flight is canceled or delayed, know what you are entitled to in terms of reimbursement, accommodation, or meal vouchers.

JOURNALING JUMP-STARTS

Do you consider yourself to be a spontaneous person? What experiences have prepared you to adapt in an unplanned adventure?

Does jumping into something new make you nervous? What traits make you feel more confident and ready to handle the unanticipated?

....

....

....

....

....

A day trip from one country to another means you'll be confronted with another unique set of rules. On your day trip, were you prepared for customs that might have differed from the country you were initially visiting? If not, how could you have prepared?

....

....

....

....

....

....

CHAPTER NINE

———

The Sensory Adventure

*It does not matter how slowly you go
so long as you do not stop.*

CONFUCIUS

I should have expected what I found as a result of wandering into my kitchen that Saturday morning. I'd been on a deadline, and all I had left by way of groceries was half a sleeve of crackers, mustard, and two eggs. Sometimes living alone means being creative with food and Uber Eats, but this was a pretty dire situation. I clearly needed to go shopping, and I decided to use that need as an opportunity for adventure.

Rather than walk to the supermarket in my neighborhood, I took advantage of the beautiful day and ventured to some of my favorite markets in Toronto. Supporting locally sourced produce and local farmers is always a treat. Also, the market stalls allow me to feel a sense of small community within my larger city. Depending on where

I am in Toronto, I patronize everything from a small Ukrainian bakery in the West End to the rows and rows of cannoli in one of Toronto's two Little Italy neighborhoods.

Yes, *two*. Little Italy at College and Yonge is a parade of Italian flags, gelato, wine, checkered tablecloths, garlic, and pizza. Corso Italia is a neighborhood with an eruption of cafés, bakeries, and trattorias, and it's an easy  streetcar ride from my house. During World Cup soccer season, the fanfare spreads all over the street, and the taverns and cafés are full.

Frequently named the Best Market in the World by *National Geographic*, St. Lawrence Market is nestled in one of the oldest neighborhoods in Toronto. Inside is produce, meat, fish, cheese, and bread from all over the world. On weekends, you're met with an entourage of a bustling crowd, shuffling through—often with their families in tow—swinging baskets and canvas bags and collecting ingredients for feasts.

I love carving out a sensory adventure in my city. No matter how small your town or city is, I guarantee an interesting sensory experience is waiting for you. It might just take some research—talking to people who have lived there for a long time, or writing to the city council, or surfing the web.

Food in My Own Backyard

Freshly baked Montreal-style bagels are one of the treats of living in a predominantly Jewish neighborhood. Prepared in a different way from the famous New York Style bagels, Montreal bagels are smaller, denser, and boiled in honey-sweetened water. Jewish delicatessens offer the best type of brunch available: the aforementioned bagels freshly baked in the dark, early hours of the morning and served with slathered cream cheese and lox. While Toronto has several chain bagel shops, including the famous Canadian Tim Hortons, independently owned shops boast the careful construction and recipes that have survived generations.

When one summer my aunt Annette traveled to Quebec for a solo camping and cycling adventure, she made it her mission to try as many mussels as she could. Anytime she was in a new restaurant in Vieux Quebec, an historical neighborhood in Quebec City, she added mussels to her order. She loved the food so much that she thought it imperative she sample as many offerings and preparations of it as possible.

As soon as I saw the title *Fromage a Trois* on Amazon, I was intrigued—more still when I learned the author of this Parisienne-set romantic comedy is a renowned food writer. The novel features a young woman who, at a crossroads in her life, leaves the safety of her family and friends to live in Paris for a year and find new work and adventures. As someone inspired by women who grab their gear and go, I loved the premise of the story. But most of all, I loved the cheese. One of the heroine's decisions is to try every type of French cheese as she spends her days walking glorious Paris. More than 365 types of cheese are on her list, one for every day of the year. (I do not recommend reading this book on an empty stomach.)

After reading the first few chapters and salivating over the savory descriptions of cheeses I had never experienced, I took a local sensory adventure to enhance my reading of the book. I wrote down the names of the cheeses I was most eager to try and set out for a day. I wanted to both read and taste. As I explored in this book's chapter on inspired adventures, books can often inform our experiences.

When I think of heightening my senses, I often think of the smell and taste of food. But I cannot forget beverages. A crisp rosé at a winery where you can taste the craft and time that went into fostering each varietal. A strong espresso. I love my Starbucks as much as the next person, but I always try to find a different caffeinated experience in a new town or city.

Food Around the World

Food festivals—much like Toronto's Ukrainian festival in the fall and the famous Taste of the Danforth in the Greek neighborhood in the East End—are prominent everywhere. On my bucket list is a trip to a state fair in the States. The carnival colors and cotton-candied world make me think of watching Hayley Mills in *Pollyanna* when I was a little girl—or small town River City, Iowa, popularized in *The Music Man* film, starring Shirley Jones and Robert Preston. My perfect state fair experience would include local cuisine—perhaps potatoes or corn on the cob, as well as some extravagantly sweet concoctions—all while fireworks and a brass band paint a world towered by colored tents and kiosks and perhaps a Ferris wheel.

Maybe you have a state fair in your home state or close by. Have you ever thought of going alone to wander and sample local preserves or baked goods and turn off the rest of the world for a while? So often, I think, dozens of sensory experiences are at our disposal, but without the prospect of a companion, we miss them.

New Orleans streets are murky with humidity in the close summer air, and yet a sense of continual narrative spins its colorful history. The beignets famed at Café du Monde in the French Quarter are a sugared pastry with the soft and gentle dough of a doughnut. Like so much of the cuisine offered in the Louisiana Cajun culture, its influence is knitted together from a few different cultures at once.

The souks in Dubai are the closest I have come to experiencing an ancient, old-world marketplace one might read about in *The Arabian Nights* or associate with the Disney film *Aladdin.*

Global Village is a massive and grand theme park between Abu Dhabi and Dubai, featuring the tastes and experiences of more than 90 international flavors. It was here that I sampled honey and dates and baklava that took me out of my usual palate and into several new experiences.

The Sensory Experience of a Ball Game

I was lucky to have two very good, third-base–side seats in the bottom level of the Rogers Centre in Toronto to see my Blue Jays play the competing Boston Red Sox. I had plans to attend with a friend, but he had to leave on a business trip at the last minute and I couldn't fill his spot. I could have sold the tickets on the internet, I suppose, but I really, *really* love any opportunity to see the Jays play in person. And these pricey seats were contest-won and a far cry from the higher levels I usually occupied with budget-conscious friends.

I knew some of my guy friends had gone to games alone—especially when out of town on a business trip. But to my girlfriends, it was almost unheard of. "Won't you feel weird?" one asked, declining the extra ticket and surprised I still intended to go. I didn't know. I hadn't done it before. So I grabbed my cap and my jersey and attended alone in a sea of blue with a few interruptions of Red Sox paraphernalia. I rose as groups of people shuffled into their seats, and I sat with my Coke—alone— and cheered the heck out of my team.

Alone, I didn't have the luxury of sharing a good play or exciting base steal or disappointing strikeout with a companion. But I took in the sights, sounds, and smells around me.

So often when I go to a baseball game, the cheers and noise and attention to the plays as well as the excitement of sharing the experience with someone keep me occupied and in adrenaline overdrive (especially in play-offs season). But solo, I had more time to focus on the music. Not just the walk-up songs preferred by the players as they approached the base but the snippets of pop, rock, and hip-hop selected to stir the crowd into cheering and to keep the energy alive during lulls in action. I studied the blasts of fluorescent advertisements high above the field and flanking the scoreboard. I smelled the popcorn and peanuts and hot dogs sold from the servers weaving in and out of the stadium rows.

All About the Sound

Sound is also integral to the experience of sensory exploration. I admit that when I wander and explore, I have a habit of keeping my earbuds in with music from my iPhone. But I still try to pay attention to the sounds around me. As a writer, I've become more aware of how I can use sound to help create a scene in a fictional piece.

It was a beautiful, crisp November day in England when I stepped off the train at the Bletchley village stop to take the short stroll to the park famed by the codebreakers who turned the tide of World War II. The grand manor house and its neighboring huts were filled with stories of codebreaking and decrypted messages as well as Alan Turing's BOMBE machine familiar to many from the film *The Imitation Game*.

My notebook, guidebook, and map were at my side, and I was listening to the commentary on the earphones provided by the museum, excited by the men and women who used math, intellect, and even chess games to intercept German messages. I wanted to visually capture as much of the action as possible to write in a forthcoming historical novel, and my iPhone was a great help as I snapped pictures and wrote short descriptions in my notes app.

Wandering through one of the huts where the group of predominantly female codebreakers spent their days in crowded, windowless spaces—humid in summer and cold in winter—I was struck by how much *noise* there was even though I was the only person roaming around at the time. I took out my notebook and wrote down the possible noises a woman who worked there might have heard in the 1940s—the radio and wired messages from telegraphs, shoes creaking on those uneven boards, people calling to one another, the sound of a typewriter, the rattle of pipes, and the pop of a stove in the winter or a badminton or ball game erupting nearby in the summer.

Something about that exercise encouraged me to spend more time tuning in to the noise around me. This doesn't necessarily mean listening in on other conversations—although in public, you can't always help but hear some of the talk around you—but hearing is a sense we can take for granted, especially in the everyday. For instance, like Henry Higgins in *My Fair Lady*, I like to see if I can differentiate accents from different parts of the world.

We often take the sound of church bells for granted too. Nearly every town and city is marked by them. Before the prevalence of personal timepieces and, of course, cell phones, church bells helped the population manage their day. In London, the bells of St Paul's Cathedral are differentiated by function: Some marked daily routine, reminding merchants and smiths and tradesmen to dismiss their apprentices for meals and then, finally, the end of a long work day, and others called for prayer.

This is not unlike the call to prayer in the United Arab Emirates, a mournful and punctuating sound that rises wherever you are in the city to tell believers it's time to either go to mosque or perform ablutions as part of the structure of the faith.

For intentional sound, I often recommend that solo travelers find a concert in a new city or town. And because choirs and chamber quartets in Prague or Budapest or Vienna often provide a free soundtrack to the bustle of pedestrian traffic, they can become part of the experience of wandering a market during one of the holy holidays. If you meander to a square or public garden, you can often find buskers and entertainers offering their musical and performing talents for tourists. Because major cities enforce licenses and hold auditions for prime spots in public spaces, these performers are often more talented than you might think. Outside Shakespeare's Globe Theatre on the south bank of the River Thames, I found a man sitting with a typewriter, clacking away and then reciting commissioned poems to tourists strolling by.

"PART OF THE EXPERIENCE OF TRAVEL— NEAR OR FAR— IS IMMERSING OURSELVES IN SIGHTS, TASTES, AND SOUNDS."

Each place has a symphony, like the wind in the trees and singing birds around Walden Pond, the El Train rambling over Chicago, the calm lap of water on shore at a lakeside retreat or cabin. Part of the experience of travel—near or far—is immersing ourselves in sights, tastes, and sounds, ensuring that we take full advantage of the experience.

Take Your Time—Even When You're Alone

The sensory adventure is best experienced slowly and with attention to detail and observation that can be well recorded in a journal. Don't be afraid to take your time just because you're on your own. There's no sense in rushing through something when your experience is best realized by teasing out the sounds and scents and sights and tastes.

Because of its proximity to the Italian border, Salzburg hosts delicious Italian restaurants, kiosks with pastries, and gelato carts. I justified eating two ice creams in the course of one morning by the amount of walking and exploring I had done through the old city center, up to the castle and to an old monastery. That was the first time I remember wondering, *Is it too early for ice cream?*

One outdoor gelato cart, bordering the gardens of Mirabell Palace—which is famed as the place where

Maria and the seven von Trapp children sing "Do Re Mi" around a stately fountain in *The Sound of Music*— became a favorite. It offered a dozen different Italian flavors, and I fell deeply in love with the Straticiatella— vanilla with chocolate shavings. *Deeply* in love. So deeply in love that I returned and returned.

The fourth time I was there during my stay, I broke into immense and unguarded praise to explain my clearly evident obsession: "My name is Rachel and I am from Canada and this is the best ice cream I have ever had in my life."

The server smiled and said, "Then this is on the house." Then he added an extra scoop to my order. I was a fervent patron, never more thankful in my life that I didn't have a dairy allergy. It was a relatively inexpensive indulgence, too, considering that while nutritionally questionable, the ice cream kept my energy up enough to see Salzburg in its ancient and musical glory.

In Graz, another Austrian city influenced heavily by Italy, I spent a muggy morning exploring the city and walking up to the famed Glockenspiel Tower overlooking spires and other towers. While my head told me to keep exploring, my heart was turned toward an outdoor Italian café bordered by the cool shade of umbrellas. Seeing and experiencing are such an integral part of any travel experience, but so is resting and taking in a moment.

I took the first intentionally leisurely lunch of my

life—starting with olives and lingering over margarita pizza, savoring each morsel of perfectly baked dough and the freshest basil and mozzarella, making out the nuance in the herbs and spices added to the tomato sauce. I paired it with lemon soda, of which I had two, and spent 90 minutes on a solo meal.

Often, when we women eat alone in a restaurant, our instinct is to rush, to eat only as a means of sustenance and necessity before hurrying off. We can feel guilty for taking up space and requiring the attention of a server. But we deserve the same experience everyone else does when dining out.

Don't hide in your phone in hopes that onlookers will assume you're merely waiting for someone. Don't hesitate to let the server know you don't need the extra set of tableware. Let the person who asks if your extra chair is available have it. But above else, don't hurry. If you rush because you're ashamed, ashamed is the vibe you'll give to others. It's empowering to instead prove to fellow diners—and to yourself—that you are good company.

Trust me. That day in Graz, I was seated solo amid several empty tables on an outdoor plaza, and I had every inclination to treat myself as if I was taking out the most splendid date.

The Cajun people are descended from the Acadian settlers who were uprooted from their homes in Nova Scotia and New Brunswick and resettled in a French-based colony in Louisiana. Just as they had to adapt to the cold Canadian winters and constant mosquitoes of Canadian summers while carving out a life in the Maritime provinces, so they had to adapt to the nearly unbearable temperatures and boggy landscape of the Louisiana swamplands. They brought several recipes with them, including the famous beignets: the doughnut-like pastries famous from Café Du Monde in the French Quarter of New Orleans.

Ingredients for Sensory Adventure

- Picnics are a treat to anyone. From a market, make a lunch out of baguettes, samples of cheese, and fresh produce.

- Watch for "mom and pop" style shops, diners, and bakeries. They're often far more reasonably priced than some of the chain restaurants so popular with tourists, and their offerings can be even more delicious.

- Look for festivals in your town or neighboring cities. Learn as much as you can about what you can sample there. You'll have to make some choices since you probably won't be able to sample it all.

- A sensory adventure is the perfect way to experience other cultures. Ask questions of the servers and workers you encounter. They'll most likely appreciate your effort to understand their trade.

- Budget for one nice restaurant in a new place. But also take advantage of street food and breakfasts built into the price of hotel stays.

- Check with your doctor about any possible clashes with medication if you plan to try new foods.

- While the temptation to overindulge might be high, consider taking small, sample sizes of new foods, recognizing that you are not necessarily used to them and your body might need some time to acclimate to them and digest them.

- At the end of the day, you still want to enjoy your trip and be healthy and ready to embark on the next adventure. If something doesn't seem appetizing, or you anticipate will make you feel less than comfortable, give yourself the gift of saying no.

- Besides amazing new food and drink experiences, consider scent. New perfume or perhaps a scented candle unique to your location will spark memories of your trip like almost nothing else. Capture the fragrance of your journey and bring it home with you when you're ready to depart.

Focus on sensory perception. Can you hear different sounds and smell a range of different flavors with the intention to clear your mind in a social setting?

....

....

....

....

Do you love a particular food? Make a list of restaurants you would like to try it in and then write a mini review in your journal.

....

....

....

....

Smell is closely linked to memory. Do you have a memory you've associated with a smell?

....

....

....

Unplug and listen. Take out your earbuds and use your sense of hearing. What do you hear? Language? Music? The sound of wheels? How does this place speak to you without words?

....

....

....

List five things you see, five things you hear, five things you smell, and five things you taste.

....

....

....

....

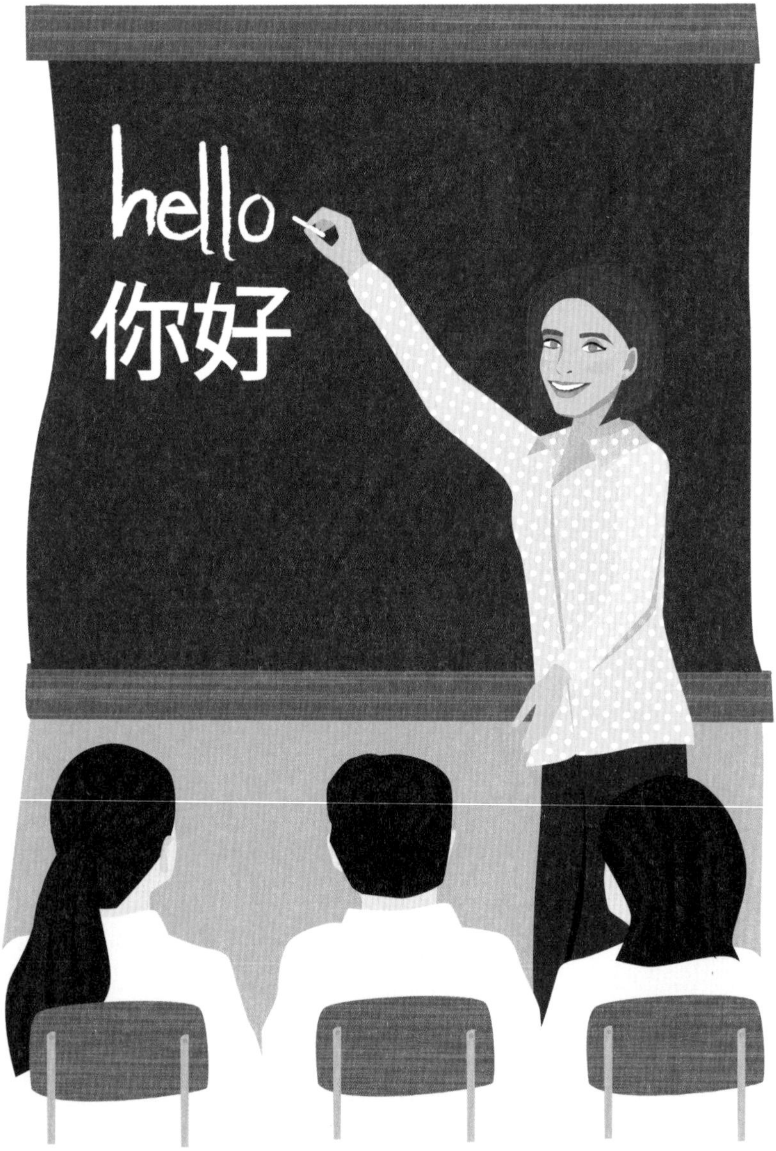
hello
你好

CHAPTER TEN

The Purposeful Adventure

The more I traveled the more I realized that fear
makes strangers of people who should be friends.

SHIRLEY MACLAINE

*Y*ou would love it here," my sister, Leah, told me on the phone, its static echo revealing how far away she was. "Every night they tell stories to each other. They put away their phones and connect the past to their present."

Leah was in Marrakesh, a city in Morocco I painted with my imagination. I thought the air must be turquoise around the Middle Eastern sun, the mosques and markets akin to stepping back centuries, the colors of wares drawing the eye while mingled spices tingled the nostrils.

Once the sun went down, the locals gathered as Leah watched.

"Could you understand them?" I asked.

"Not a word. It was all in Arabic. But I could tell how

enraptured they were. They were captivated. They were connected."

The culture and customs and history of this ancient place lived on through young and old gathering to tell stories, and in a world of flashing phone notifications and people searching for Wi-Fi, Leah connected by disconnecting—even with the barrier of language. Visual cues, body language, and the rapt attention of dozens of eyes on an animated storyteller were all the narrative this purposeful traveler needed.

My purposeful adventures have been either for my education or for research trips that inspire and provide context for the historical fiction I write. So far they have taken me to places where I've felt relatively safe and could adapt, and my preparation for them took a different commitment than working with embassies and scheduling consultation about malaria pills. But just because all purposes aren't the same doesn't mean they're not all important experiences. Comparison has no place. All adventures are equal when we're challenged and inspired by them. Stories need not tip the scale in favor of the daring traveler who has ridden an elephant in Indonesia, or been on a high wire in Mexico, or even helped to build a church or school with her own hands. If you've undertaken an adventure and traveled—near or far—for a purpose, your story matters.

The next best thing to personal adventure is hearing about other people's adventures, much like hearing Leah tell about absorbing words in Marrakesh that she tucked away along with those rapt faces and the sound of silent cell phones. Here's more about Leah's story and two others.

Leah and Africa

Leah's purposeful travel has found her deep in consultation work in villages that look nothing like the safe Canadian town we grew up in. She's spent years so immersed in African cultures for her research on education and global initiatives that she speaks passable Swahili. The latter, as well as the native wraparound she wore while climbing Mount Kilimanjaro, earned her the moniker "Mama Africa" from the locals.

"People appreciate it when travelers make the attempt to engage with their culture," she explained when I asked her to give some advice on traveling purposefully. Leah told me that appreciation doesn't mean automatic assimilation or acceptance of views or religions. Rather, it's an extension of the humility purposeful travelers should have as they respectfully integrate into other cultures. The guides on her trek up Mount Kilimanjaro found in Leah a spirit of humility, an admission of vulnerability, a care and passion for the culture and community.

Jessica and China

An unforeseen career change found my friend Jessica at the crux of opportunity: She could either search for employment immediately or teach English overseas. Because travel presented a way to not only work but also 你好 learn a new culture and language, she decided to teach in China, gaining a new perspective of the culture. Then she carried that purposeful adventure into taking further lessons in the language when she returned home, a way to extend the influence of her experience as she integrated back into the North American workforce.

Hannah and El Salvador

My cousin Hannah's return to Canada from El Salvador found her not only wanting to connect to the culture she'd left behind but also to help some of the women who became a part of her story during her purposeful adventure. She'd developed a love for the local and historical practice of making pupusa, a stuffed cornmeal flatbread, and with little effort for the exponential gain, she made it for a backyard fundraiser to help a single mother who had woven herself into Hannah's experience. Connected to the culture from afar, she offered a flavor of what she'd experienced in a place she felt affinity with and still misses between trips.

Purposeful adventures take women to places that leave them with a keen desire to instill that adventure right where they are. They also allow women to contribute to a larger story that makes the world a smaller place. Jessica continued her language classes. Leah learned how to make her favorite Ghanaian dishes with ingredients available in North America. Hannah held a fundraiser. Tutoring Syrian refugees, supporting a night of traditional Ethiopian cuisine, offering an email of advice to students preparing for their own purposeful adventure… there is always a way to continue the adventure at home.

Of the women I spoke to about solo purposeful travel, some did so in pursuit of a degree, others to make money, many for a calling. All who had undertaken these adventures had the same advice for those attempting the same: Remember, it's easy to *assume* that you'll simply arrive in a different country and teach or instill something in the people there, leaving your mark on the world. But instead, you'll leave having *learned*.

The Role of Humility

I asked Leah what she would tell someone who was planning to travel purposefully, especially overseas.

"Each community has a story," Leah explained. "You can't paint an entire country or continent with one stroke. You have to narrow in. Experience. Appreciate."

The savviest sojourner recognizes that thoughtful and appreciative travel results in the world becoming a smaller place and the traveler's life being far more enriched for the experience. But one word sticks out to Leah as being the most resonant for all travel—whether going overseas or making a trip much closer to home.

"Humility," she told me without taking a breath or a beat. "Cultivate humility before you leave and after you arrive."

Humility is a word I write again and again, certain that its influence reaches far beyond planned solo adventure. But not just for adventure. For engagement. The more I learn from others' stories, the more I appreciate and enjoy their Facebook albums and their scrolling through their photos, the more I feel connected to those with an adventurous spirit. My heart beats a little faster and my bucket list get a little longer.

In every adventure, a humble spirit and a willingness to engage and learn opens the possibility of a smaller world.

*P*upusa was created centuries ago by the Pipil tribe that inhabited the territory now known as El Salvador. Discovered ancient cooking tools for their preparation have led archaeologists to believe these flatbreads have been made for almost 2,000 years in local regions. Passed down from generation to generation, instruction and recipes for pupusa are the food equivalent of a narrative story that withstands years and cultural shifts.

Prepare for a New Culture

- All cultures appreciate it when visitors have done their homework. Learn a word or two about the language, learn about a food, and learn a custom. A little goes a long way to show respect.

- Consult an expert or reach out to the affiliation you're traveling for or with to gain a thorough, firsthand perspective about the culture you'll be visiting.

- Understand the history of the place you're visiting. Every country is shaped by context, and its history and narrative defines its customs. From colonization to wars, a keen understanding of the history will prepare you to engage with the locals.

- If you're traveling alone, ask another woman for directions or advice to get the female perspective.

- Each country has different rules about social media and photography. Ensure that you know the laws regarding media.

- Rather than take tours that are merely consumptive of a culture, take a cooking or yoga class to truly experience the flavor of a faraway place.

- If there is a restaurant or shop in your city or town featuring foods or goods from the part of the world you're heading to, visit beforehand and ask the owners your questions about the culture and traditions.

- Learn the customs for what is considered "modest" or "appropriate" dress for women. It differs from country to country.

- This may seem obvious, but take your patience along with you when you travel to a foreign place. Some customs or rules in a different culture may seem unnecessarily difficult or confusing, especially when you're in a time zone you're not use to, but a smile, a gracious attitude, and being open to adjusting some of the things you take for granted will go a long way to making your adventure much easier, more fun, and more comfortable.

JOURNALING JUMP-STARTS

Write down all your preconceived notions about the place you're visiting purposefully before you go. Then compare your notes to how things are different than anticipated.

What did you think you'd be teaching or imparting to the people you were visiting on a purposeful adventure? Instead, what did you learn?

....

....

....

....

....

....

....

....

....

....

....

....

....

....

....

....

....

....

CHAPTER ELEVEN

The Daring Adventure

To live is the rarest thing in the world.
Most people exist, that is all.

OSCAR WILDE

My social media erupted as suddenly as the blaze across my TV screen had. Notre Dame Cathedral was on fire, and a newscaster was attempting to report the event in real time. When the blaze was out, the bell towers, relics, and some of the foundations and windows remained intact, but it will take upward of a generation to restore the church's past glory.

As the roof was licked with flames, the medieval spiral finally toppling across the smoky sky, I noticed that one group of people—the experienced—clogged my feeds with photos and stories, hashtags and recollections, some from decades ago. They praised their time in Paris and mourned the grand landmark of one of the world's most beautiful cities. Others—the inexperienced—who had always longed to see the grand cathedral in person, commented as they watched the blaze threaten to take away the opportunity they craved. They mourned the adventure they'd never taken, the fact that a grand structure on their bucket list would never again be as they dreamed and imagined. They grieved even as they voiced regret for the loss of history and art.

On that horrible day, family members sent me texts with condolences and thoughts as though I'd experienced a death. And I suppose I had. Often, solo adventure prompts us to feel an affinity to a place and personify the same deep feelings we might have for a human being.

But what better metaphor to inspire us to dare, to go—even alone?

What can inspire us to save for a grand bucket list adventure alone? What might we cut back on in daily life or replace to achieve a larger goal? How can business-trip airline points or discount deals or asking for travel funds for birthday and Christmas gifts translate into a dream realized?

Not everyone has the means or time to travel far, of course. But what local bucket list can dare us? What opportunities on a smaller scale might propel us to grab at a solo chance to experience life on our own terms? *Daring* is a word that need not be saved just for climbing Mount Everest—though those brave enough to do so inhabit that word fully. But we can dare on smaller scales. For you, daring might mean going *anywhere* alone. Or if you're like me, it might mean doing something that frightens you. Facing heights, for example.

Standing at the Bottom

The train trip to Meiringen was a moving postcard of snowcapped mountains and crisp blue seas, trademarks of the Interlaken district of Switzerland. For this Sherlock Holmes fan, the prospect of seeing the famed Reichenbach Falls, where Holmes supposedly perished alongside his nemesis, Professor Moriarty, in Sir Arthur Conan Doyle's short story "The Adventure of the Final Problem," was thrilling. Upon arrival, I explored the village, snapped pictures of the chalet-style houses, ate cabbage and fritters at a mountainside café, and purchased a Sherlock Holmes T-shirt at a gift shop/museum amid streets with names like Holmestrasse and Conan Doyle Platz. Then it was time to see what I'd most anticipated.

My pre-trip internet study had informed me that a half-hour hike would lead me to the bottom of the famous falls, from which I could take a funicular railway to the top. I have never been great with heights, but I had long dreamt of making an exception for this important literary excursion.

The funicular, I saw upon approach, was not unlike a rickety wooden cart employed by Wile E. Coyote in pursuit of the Road Runner. The conveyance, I saw from my vantage point safely at the bottom, was an open and exposed wooden cart, and it chugged along a sketchy track up, up, up to the top of the falls. (Men were working on the track with hammer and nail once one funicular got back in preparation for the next.) There were no railings—just this open wooden cart and tracks up the rock. Something else of note: An aptly placed hospital sat at the foot of the mountain, I assumed to give solace to those who thought plummeting down that rock wouldn't necessarily end in their death.

Deciding I didn't fancy perishing or at the very least having a full-blown episode wherein I would shout, "Let me out! Let me out!" halfway up the track, I snapped a few pictures and turned away, sure I had saved my life.

But I hadn't dared. I'd backed out. The imagination that had painted the scene so clearly to me wouldn't allow me to see anything but sudden death when faced with the challenge of going up the mountain.

Later, after catching the train back to my hotel in Zurich, I berated myself for losing my nerve. I was so sure I was going to seize this moment to overcome my fear of heights. What more magnanimous triumph than reaching the top of the stunning Reichenbach Falls? But instead, my daring adventure had become another example of letting my fear get the better of me. The photographs I imagined taking from the top before proudly calling my family and friends to let them know that I *did* it had gone beyond any assumption that height-scared Rachel would back out.

There is grace when we admit our limitations and experience fear in vulnerable moments. The solo adventure should stretch us, but we're still going to be ourselves. The best adventures allow us to get to know ourselves better, but often how we are, not how we would like to be.

Yet sometimes independent adventure encourages us to step out of our comfort zones, to take a risk. Sure, sometimes we get lonely or miss home, especially if a time difference makes it difficult to call or FaceTime the people in our lives. Sometimes we experience culture shock. Sometimes we run into hurdles and are baffled and challenged, but the risk can be worth taking.

Remember the cab driver in Prague who said he wouldn't let me out until I paid his inflated fare? After I gave him the money and left the taxi, I climbed the stairs to my second-floor hotel room deflated, ashamed that I hadn't been able to control the situation. But it was just

*"THE BEST
ADVENTURES
ALLOW US TO
GET TO KNOW
OURSELVES
BETTER."*

a moment when I chose to back down. I determined to keep enjoying my time in the city. I didn't let the shadow of a help-less experience get me down. My well-being meant more than my assertion that I was in the right. I was fortunate to be safe and ready to explore. I dared to go on.

Sometimes the daring adventure we've planned will end with our looking up at the Reichenbach Falls from the safety of the ground below. Sometimes we just *can't*. But other times we adventure far harder than we thought ourselves capable.

Standing at the Top

The 387 steps to get to the top of the North and South towers of Notre Dame in Paris are narrow and dark, suffo-cating in their steep twists and turns. Let's just say there's probably a good reason Victor Hugo's bell ringer, Quasi-modo, stayed up with the bells most of his life.

I not only don't have a great history with scary heights; I also don't have a great history with confined spaces. Case in point, I made a jumble of the single-file line up to the famous Blarney Stone at Blarney Castle in Ireland when I backed out midway up, forcing a bit of a reverse domino situation. And a noisy bird scared me into nearly toppling over the tower's rail at the top of the

Prasna Brana in Prague, down onto the Instagram-worthy spires and rooftops.

But I was determined to make it up Notre Dame's dizzying spiral staircase. The two tiny Italian kids in front of me were terrified of my resting scowl (I later apologized in a strange hybrid of English and Italian with flailing hand gestures demonstrating how scared I was—and they laughed), and the squeaky voice of the impatient teenage boy behind me did little to calm my shaky nerves. But I did it, at my own pace and focused on my goal.

Once at the top, I stepped out to greet the parapets guarded by saints and gargoyles ushering the grand views to each district of the historic city, beyond the Seine to the Eiffel Tower. I was prouder than if I had been with someone who had championed me. Prouder because no one knew I had accomplished that feat in the moment but me. I had no cheerleader but myself and the knowledge that I had overcome a great obstacle.

Now I stood, snapping photos and taking a well-deserved moment while people crowded on either side, urging my heart to beat while experiencing claustrophobia and realizing very little stood between me and a quick drop hundreds of feet to the ground. I dared, and I did, and the experience was all the more significant in my independent pursuit.

Dare to Go

You can't align daring with only those who have done so to a certain extreme. Daring means something different for all of us. For some, conquering fear does mean a feat like climbing Mount Kilimanjaro. For others, it means taking the subway for the first time— or as I said before, going anywhere alone. For some, daring is equivalent to walking the Camino de Santiago pilgrimage in Spain while others are empowered registering for a marathon or retreat alone in a neighboring city.

What we all can do—universally—is appreciate the opportunities we've had, learn from them, and remain open to more if we're so inclined to take them. We can all be daring.

Grab your gear and go. Step out of your comfort zone. Face your fears. Book a night for that movie you want to see because you've heard the cinematography is grand. Make a reservation for one at the restaurant in a nearby neighborhood serving an international cuisine your husband or friends aren't partial to. And if, unlike me, your daring runs toward the extreme, go hang gliding or climb a mountain. Chase the skies.

In *The Music Man*, swindling salesman Harold Hill tells stiff librarian Marian Paroo, "If you pile up enough tomorrows, you'll find you've collected nothing but a lot of empty yesterdays." I don't want empty yesterdays. I want moments when I've been vulnerable or stupid or strong. I want to have tried that dish on the menu that walked a fine line between interesting and disgusting. I want to have seen that community production of a play clearly produced because the rights were dirt cheap. I want to have some daring adventures.

I also remain a hopeless romantic. My dashing prince hasn't arrived on my doorstep either in a white horse-drawn carriage or Volvo, but I have never once shelved a dream or experience while waiting for him to arrive. And I have pockets full of amusing anecdotes to splice through the silence when I sit across from a stranger as the first awkward moments of our date tick by. I *dare* to be a romantic in the traditional sense. I *dare* to value my dreams and interests.

And I dare *you* to do the same. I *double* dare you.

*A*uthor Victor Hugo was inspired to write *The Hunchback of Notre Dame* to make his contemporaries aware of the value of Gothic architecture in an age when many Gothic structures in Paris were falling into disrepair or had been destroyed in pursuit of the newer styles popularized by grand new buildings throughout the city. This is partly why the book's plot is balanced by long descriptions about the cathedral, from its gargoyles to its crypts and stained glass.

Money and Budgeting

- Have fun making your dream destination a reality, but be intentional about when you go. You don't want to be stressed financially.

- Off-seasons differ by location. If you're choosing to experience an off-season deal to save money, ensure that everything you wanted to experience at your destination is open.

- Using a website like Expedia to book a day trip or tour while at your destination is a great way to save some money (as well as feel less alone).

- Make sure your credit card provider knows you're going away so they won't freeze your card because of unusual account activity. You can also ask about potential fees if you use a debit or credit card in a foreign location.

- Be your own travel agent. When reading online reviews of a hotel, airline, or experience (TripAdvisor is a great place to start), read a wide variety and assess based on a curve. Don't let a one-star review from a bitter traveler keep you from looking carefully at the way the establishment responds to negative comments as well as the reviews from 4- and 5-star reviewers. Be savvy enough to know when to take critical reviews with a grain of salt, and then choose a place within your budget.

- Weeks before you go, watch the exchange rates closely (online at a site such as XE Currency Converter) and request your currency, as per your bank's policies, when it looks like you'll get the most bang for your buck.

- Book as much as you can in your own currency before you go. Expedia is one example of a travel site that allows you to purchase events in your currency, to be redeemed when you arrive at your destination.

- Several cities have packages for theaters and concerts combined with a dinner. Book packages as much as you can to save money, budget wisely, and save yourself additional expense when you get there.

Write down what experience you would remark on if you had someone by your side.

....

....

....

....

....

....

....

....

....

....

What did you notice when you were alone that might not have stood out had you been with another person or in a group?

....

....

....

....

....

....

....

....

....

....

....

....

....

....

....

Let's Go on an Adventure

*I*f we were sitting across from each other, perhaps drinking *Einspanner* at the Café Mozart in Vienna, I would remind you that life experiences inform tenets of courage. Being single requires me to live life and its experiences primarily alone. And although I grew up in a small town, I moved to the fourth most populated city in North America, making me accustomed to a large metropolitan area. Neither of those facts unique to me, however, have created a better dreamer or planner or independent traveler than you can be.

By now, you should know that I believe dreaming and planning and going need not involve the investment of overseas travel or the call to a purposeful adventure. It can mean going to a matinee, ordering a latte, seeing a movie under the stars, visiting a place in your own backyard. As much as I want to encourage women to believe they deserve the opportunity of their own company, deserve to look at life romantically whether or not that romance includes another person, and find the confidence to do these things, I most want them to turn off the world long enough to know who they are. To get to know themselves beyond the noise and chaos of a world with Snapchat and Facebook.

That means spending time alone. You are who you truly are when no one else is around, with no expectation of conversation, with no tailoring of your thoughts and phrases to suit an experience with other people.

At the end of the day, you are your own happily ever after. Maybe some part of you feels you're not enough, that you need someone with you no matter what—a friend or boyfriend or husband. Perhaps that's because you don't yet see what enough looks like for you. But you can learn what's enough for you when you get to know yourself.

Validate and respect yourself by acknowledging your interests and pursuing them, with or without a companion. We don't often hesitate to invest time and money in an experience or gift to please someone else, and that's wonderful. But there's nothing wrong in forging our own path or trying something new for ourselves. Aren't we

"YOU ARE
WHO YOU TRULY
ARE WHEN
NO ONE ELSE IS
AROUND."

worth the investment as well?

I'm not suggesting we sacrifice responsibility to family. Nor am I suggesting that we throw off everything in our lives and reroute to the edge of the world. I'm just hoping that we all find reasonable ways to carve out time to treasure ourselves. I'm encouraging at least an evening, or a day, or a weekend to do that. With all the time meted for jobs and family and friends, why not splice a little bit for us? It's perfectly okay to carve out time for the dreams and desires of your heart that may not have other people in them. It's also natural to want to have experiences on your own, just as it's natural to have moments of reservation.

Certainly, comfort and security come in having people around you, and we might associate *alone* with distant and cold. But alone time can help us better relate to the people in our lives because we can use it to recharge and grow. It can also enrich our lives in ways we might not have imagined. For instance, the historical snapshots included in this book are those I have collected from years of reading and travel. In keeping with the hopeful, conversational tone, I merely relayed stories and facts I already knew. I may not be able to pinpoint exactly how I know them, but they are tidbits that stick like Velcro in my heart and memory due to my excitement in learning new things.

How different would a day planned with the closest people in your life look from a day planned just for yourself? Would you tweak a few of your desires for the sake of a common decision or compromise? Would you find yourself backing down from something you want to do—however insignificant—because it doesn't appeal to your companions? What about that movie playing that no one in your family or circle of friends wants to see? Does your family hate spicy foods while you crave Indian? A healthy selfishness isn't putting yourself *above* others; it's recognizing that you also deserve the opportunity to grab an opportunity for yourself.

Don't be afraid to have adventures for yourself—big and small. All bravery is worthy of recognition, measured on different but equal scales. Brave can mean simply stepping out of your comfort zone.

My greatest hope in writing this book is that some woman, somewhere, will read it and then do something new. That she'll grab an opportunity to spend time on her own. That she'll dream, plan, and go.

About the Author

Rachel McMillan is the author of the Herringford and Watts mysteries, the Three Quarter Time series of contemporary romances set in opulent Vienna, and the Van Buren and DeLuca mysteries. Her upcoming historical series is set in postwar Europe amid some of the world's most beautiful churches. Rachel lives in Toronto, Canada, and is always planning her next adventure.

Connect with Rachel:

www.rachelmcmillan.net

dream,
plan,
& go

Adventure Journal

with helpful travel tips from

RACHEL McMILLAN

ARTWORK *by* LAURA BEAN

You dreamt, you planned, you went. Now what?

Celebrate your travel triumphs and the lessons learned along the way in this one-of-a-kind companion journal. So much more than just blank space to write down your thoughts, you will discover daily entry pages that help you memorialize the people, places, and things you've experienced during your excursions.

The journal is packed with practical advice for smart traveling that will help you make the most of every adventure you embark on, both big and small.

There's a great big world waiting for you—go find it!

HARVEST HOUSE PUBLISHERS
EUGENE, OREGON

HarvestHousePublishers.com

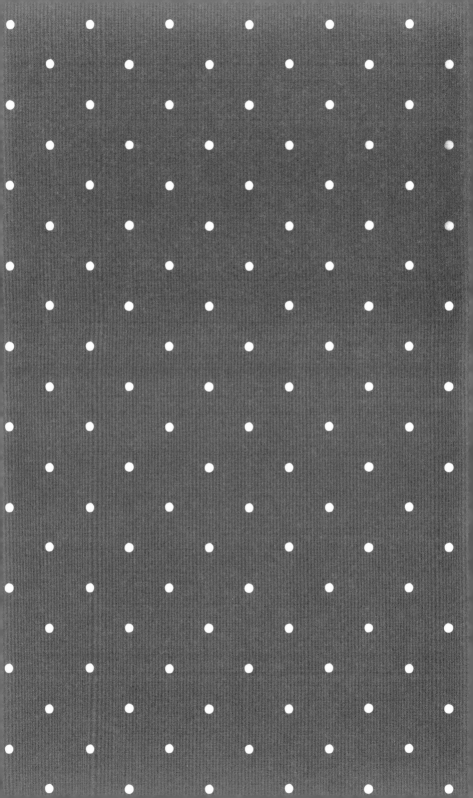

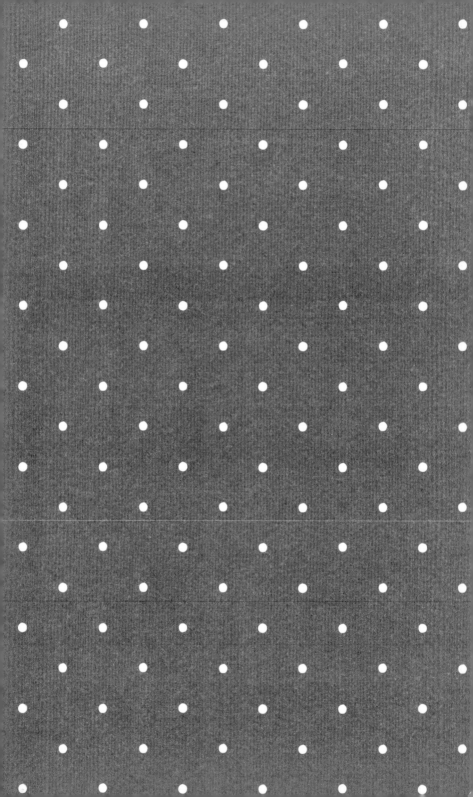